TRACKS

Memoirs of a Vietnam Veteran

By Sergeant Clyde Hoch
of the United States Marine Corps

A Marine in Vietnam
By Frank Carr

I was barely eighteen when I became a United States Marine.
They quickly made me into a killing machine.
They sent me halfway across the world to tempt my fate
before then I'd never even been out of State.
We couldn't tell friend from foe.
From village to jungle to rice paddies we did go in search of
our enemy or so we were told to kill those commies wher-
ever they're hold.
Don't shoot unless you're shot at.
What kind of a war is that?
With our big tanks we went out cruising to turn the peasant's
rice crop into ruin.
We were told to be ambassadors these people are our host.
But at night they'd sneak up quiet as a ghost to sing their
song of the Viet Cong with bombs and bullets and then be
gone only to return and fight on yet another night.
I see an old man; he's wearing white they said.
Take him out he's in your sight.
I fired the canon and watched its red flight straight as an ar-
row with a terrible might.
My heart turned to stone but my Captain said son it's alright
for this is a free kill zone.
I see a young man walking quietly engaged.
Then getting blown away by a hand grenade.
I see a tree line it's just ahead.
But the battle field before me littered with dead.
Our tanks move in blasting and onward we go to overrun and
kill our enemy foe.
We never lost a battle not one time around.
But then we would leave and give back the ground.
I'm at the end of my tour my Country's in dissention.
Then why have I signed up for a six month extension?
It's for sure I don't like to fight.
But I'm still convinced what we're doing is right.
One thing I cannot quite figure is how the memories do so
linger from the past so far away from a war misbegotten that
should be forgotten but just seems with me to stay.
The stench of death lingers longly.
For a war that went oh, so wrongly.

Dedication

This book is dedicated to all of my brothers who fell and rose back up, but were never whole again.

Once when visiting a friend in the hospital in the states, I saw a vet strapped to a bed. He had no legs or arms. There was a very beautiful woman talking to him and a cute little girl with the lady. I assumed it was his wife and daughter. I almost choked on that one. I cannot come close to thinking what life was like for him and his wife.

Acknowledgements

Thank you, reader, for taking the time out of your life to venture into a piece of my history. May you find wisdom, understanding, and compassion in your life, as I have found in mine.

I want to acknowledge all of the people who made this book possible. Gary and Margie Mefford, David Forsyth, Daniel Ramey, and Cathy Stapleton for their editing efforts. Gary, Todd, Ralph, Frank, Jim and David, who added their own experiences and assisted with the technical information when my memory was hazy. And lastly, Tina Simmons who worked without complaint (almost) through many edits, changes, and additions, waiting patiently for me to declare the book complete. I am also grateful to her for completing the design and layout of the book. Without Tina's assistance, this book would never have made it to print.

Mostly, thank you to all of the men who fought by my side and who had my back. I would not be here if it was not for your bravery and courage. You are all heroes.

Introduction

My name is Sergeant Clyde Hoch of C Company, First Tank Battalion, First Marine Division, Fleet Marine Force. I served in Vietnam from February of 1968 to April of 1969. Statistically, I am one of 2,709,918 Americans who actually served in the Vietnam War. Less than 850,000 of us are estimated to be alive today. We are dying at a much higher rate than the average person who did not serve in Vietnam.

This book is not just about me. It is about the millions of men and women who left their loving families to do whatever was necessary to protect our way of life. They came from all walks of life and filled positions within the military. They were cooks, clerks, and combat infantry. They did their country a great service regardless of their military function or branch of service.

Once they left the military, they returned to an ordinary life as a factory worker, construction worker, school teacher, policeman, or even an actor. They became ordinary people with ordinary jobs but kept the horrendous memory of war tucked away in their hearts and minds. Some of their friends and relatives had no idea of the memories. Some did not care. Bless all of you who served our country throughout the ages, without concern for your life but for the betterment of our country.

I felt TRACKS was an appropriate title for my journey since I spent most of my time in the Marine Corps with the tanks, however, the title is two-fold, as this book is about the tracks that I have left in my life. I believe it to be an appropriate caption to the stories, emotions, and memories that have contributed thus far to my life's journey. Tracks speaks to my accomplishments as well as the many mistakes that have served me as lessons learned. It speaks to the beautiful gifts I have been given, the struggles that have nudged me along the way, and encouraged me to grow - mentally, spiritually, and emotionally, My life, like all of our lives, has been a series of trials and tribulations, triumphs and failure. We have many memories, thoughts, and stories that make up our history. This is a part of my history.

Table of Contents

Eighteen

Eighteen. It is the age of promise. Eighteen is when we are legally adults but mentally just beginning to understand what that really means. What were you doing when you were eighteen years old? Were you planning to learn the family business or go as far from your family as possible? Maybe you were planning to go to Community College, Penn State, or Yale, to become a teacher, salesman, or psychologist? Were you getting married, having a baby, or strapping a guitar to your back and heading to California? Maybe you are not eighteen yet and you are just now starting to contemplate your path into the future. Eighteen is filled with fear, hope, anticipation, anxiety, expectations, freedom, and responsibility. Eighteen is when most of us celebrate our high school graduation and start thinking about the rest of our lives. At eighteen I was heading off to war. When I was eighteen I volunteered for the hard, fast track in becoming a man; for it was then that I was introduced to the United States Marine Corps.

Most of the people I was fighting side by side with were eighteen years old. Some of the staff and officers were much older, but most of the fighting force were eighteen and just out of high school. There was a saying in the Nam, "If you were rich, you went to college. If you were poor, you went to the Nam."

> 61% of the men killed in Vietnam were 21 or younger...11,465 of those killed were younger than 20 years old.
>
> Five men killed in Vietnam were only 16 years old.

Growing Up

In high school I never had any real goals. I was from a poor family in a small town. I always knew that I would end up serving in the military.

In my neighborhood the children always got together and played Army. We had huts and forts. Washington street served as a dividing line. The guys below it were the Brooklyn gang and we just called ourselves the Pennsburg gang. Anyone living on the Brooklyn side was our enemy. Anyone on our side of the street was our friend. If you were caught checking out the enemies territory, you were a prisoner and subject to their rules which included being bound and gagged. Of course, they could beat you for information which you were not allowed to give under any circumstances.

We sometimes had mud ball fights and apple battles. A weed that grew in the area made a decent spear when it was dried out. We had a large hut in a huge willow tree. It was built and added on to by several generations, and now it was ours. It was like a sacred place for us. On the other side of the street, the enemy had a really cool hut. It was a rectangular shape with a door and windows. The hut was made from brush and small trees found nearby. Its frame was tied and nailed in places to hold it together. It was large enough to hold about twelve kids.

I was second youngest in our group. That was bad for me. The one person that I hung out with the most was the youngest of our group (who was later killed in Vietnam). His older brother was our leader so they went easier on him. I, however, had no one to protect me. My big brother was in Germany in the real Army at the time. As I said, there was no real question if I would go into the military upon graduation from high school. One of the older kids in our group went into the Marines. I didn't really know what the Marines were all about back then.

Sometime later, some of the guys got older and more interested in girls than playing Army. Due to lack of interest, we younger guys combined our forces. We were now one big group - the Brooklyn gang and the Pennsburg gang were now all friends. Now we had to pick sides - who would be the enemy and who would be the good guys.

My big brother was coming home from Germany. The whole neighborhood turned out to greet him. They made a cake for him. It was the biggest celebration I had ever seen in our little neighborhood. I remember him walking down the street with his uniform on, carrying his sea bag, walking as straight as could be. What a hero he was! I was very proud of him.

In my last two years of high school I started reading books on Patton, MacArthur, and famous generals from World War II. Then I picked up a book on Chesty Puller, a Marine Corps General. What a general he was! He made sure the lowest ranking men got served first at the mess hall. He once saw a man saluting an officer over and over. He asked the officer what was going on. The officer said, "This man didn't salute me when I passed him, so I am making him salute me one thousand times."

General Puller said, "That's fine, but, every time this man salutes you, you will return the salute."

Now I wanted to learn more about the Marines! They seemed so noble. The one person from the Brooklyn side of the neighborhood who enlisted in the Marines came home on leave. He came to visit me and told me all these cool stories. I was hooked. I always looked up to him. If he did something, I would follow him - as was the case with going into the Marines.

I had heard about Vietnam. There was a draft in effect at that time and I knew I would be drafted into the army. Near the end of high school, three of us went to see a Marine recruiter and took the tests. One of the guys backed out, and the other one did not pass the test. So three months before I graduated, I was the only one who enlisted. I was committed to the military before I ever left high school. I felt so cool! It was exciting! I was going to be a Marine! I knew it would not be easy, and I wondered if I would be able to make it.

Three days after graduation, I was off to Parris Island, leaving behind a girlfriend, a family, friends, and the only life I had ever known.

Boot Camp

I was off to Parris Island, South Carolina only three days after I graduated from high school. The people living east of the Mississippi went to Parris Island for boot camp training. The people west of the Mississippi (for the most part) went to San Diego. We used to call them Hollywood Marines.

This was my first real time away from home and the first time being around so many people I did not know. That alone was frightening to me.

What a shock boot camp was! We arrived in the middle of the night. As soon as the bus stopped, drill instructors climbed aboard and started yelling in our ears. It seemed like it did not stop for three months. On our first morning, after only a couple hours of sleep, three drill instructors snuck into the barracks. One turned on the light. Then all three made as much noise as possible throwing metal trash cans and yelling at the top of their voices. What a fun way to wake up. It scared the hell out of me. They conditioned us so much that as soon as the light was turned on, you would leap out of your rack (bed). We would have to stand at attention at the end of our rack, holding our sheet and pillow in front of us. I was never sure what that was all about. I assume it was to check for stains, just to make it harder to make your rack, or both.

I remember we were given ten minutes to make our rack. (remake the spring bed we slept in), visit the head (men's room), shave, shower, brush our teeth, get dressed and be standing in formation out in front of the barracks. Heaven forbid you were the last person there. There would be a punishment of some kind. Our racks were usually stacked two high so you had to compete with the guy making up the other rack, upper or lower, to get yours done. Thank God for our Marine Corps haircuts! We didn't have enough hair to comb, which saved us a lot of time. There were no combs in Boot Camp.

We were allowed no television, smokes, candy, or gum. Letters were quickly sent home saying not to sneak any gum in a letter. I witnessed many men eating a letter along with the gum inside. Yes they had to eat the envelope, letter inside, and gum. We were not allowed to speak unless spoken to by a DI (drill instructor). Every reply would have to start with "SIR" and most times end with "SIR". You know - "SIR! YES SIR!"

We had an hour of free time every day towards the evening. In this free time, we had to write a letter home, shine our boots and brass, shower, brush our teeth, and get prepared for the next day. We had to really rush to get everything done.

All photos of girlfriends or anything that was even remotely considered risque were taken away and given back at the end of boot camp. I think they did it so we would keep our focus on becoming a Marine.

At the beginning of boot camp, we had to walk through a line to get shots in our arms. We felt like cattle in a shoot. We would walk through and sometimes get up to four shots at once. Then we would go back the next day for more. They gave us cards telling us what shots we received. Come to think of it, I do not ever recall anyone getting so much as a cold the whole time I was in the service.

After a week or so, the DI said that we could have a smoke, "If you have them, grab them, and go out to the smoking rack". That was where we washed our own clothes. It was a large concrete sink with faucets along the back of it. It also had buckets hanging along the rack to serve as butt cans. After meeting out there, he would say, "Light them if you got them". I remember getting off one puff and the DI said, "Put them out." That was it, after all that time, one puff. As time progressed, we were allowed to finish a smoke. Soon we were permitted up to four smokes a day, if we did very well that day. We had to field strip a cigarette, which was knock the hot ash off the end, make sure it was out by crushing it with your fingers, and put the remains in your pocket.

I was in boot camp June, July, and August. It was hot as hell, but that didn't prevent us from running. I remember going on runs where when we returned, we could literally ring the sweat out of our shirts as if they were soaking in water. Sometimes we ran out for quite some time, then started back towards the barracks. I would be so happy thinking, "Thank God! It's almost over! I could see our barracks! We are finally finished!" And then we would go right past the barracks. It would piss me off so bad! Almost as bad as being woken up the way we were.

There was a flag system. Some days the DI would tell someone to go out and see what flag was flying. Apparently if it was a red flag the DI had to be careful of giving us heat exhaustion. Once the report came back that it was a black flag (the black flag meant it was too hot to do anything). The DI said, "I can't make you do any drills or exercise where anyone can see you. So we will stay inside and exercise with foot locker drills." The dreaded foot locker drills! We did rifle drills using our foot lockers as rifles. When we went to dinner that evening, we were told to march out of step because it was too hot to march in step. I was not certain as to the difference, but that is what we were ordered to do. We were on a need to know basis, and I guess we didn't need to know why. This would be a reoccurring theme in my Marine Corps career.

Heaven forbid you called your rifle a gun or your trousers pants. Some of the guys who called their rifle a gun would sometimes have to sleep with it or would have to shout many times, "This is my rifle, this is my gun (pointing to his groin), this is for fighting this is for fun." The response to pants was, "Only women and sailors wore pants."

Once, in boot camp, while standing at attention one of the guys looked to see a fire truck go by. The DI caught him looking and made him hold two buckets of water straight out in his arms running around the squad bay yelling like a fire truck.

We marched and ran so much in the beginning that it was hard not to get blisters on your feet. We always wore the high black leather boots. When we got blisters, we were sent to sick bay. In the mornings, the DI would call out, "Sick, lame, and lazy fall out". If we needed to go to sick bay, we were allowed. We were marched over by another DI. I went once for a blister and was told, "Go back, you will be fine". I had blister upon blister. They eventually went away and were replaced by thick calluses.

It was customary to hold the door open for the DI until he went through. Single doors were no problem. At sick bay there was a double glass door. Now I faced a dilemma - there were two doors and they were spaced about eight feet apart. Now what do I do? I held the first door opened until the DI got there. I let it go and it slammed into him. I ran and opened the second door for him. As he passed through the second door he said, "If you ever let a door slam on me again I will kill you!" I felt like a dumb ass.

On Sundays, we had the morning off. We had our choice of cleaning the barracks or going to church. There were not too many atheists at boot camp.

The rule of the mess hall was simple - we could take all the food we wanted, but we had better eat everything we took. I used to drink so much at dinner that I would get sick to my stomach. It was so hot, and I was always so thirsty that I would drink rather than eat much. Once, on the way back from the mess hall, I got sick to my stomach. I was going to hurl. I asked the DI for permission to speak. He granted it. I asked him to break formation because I was going to hurl. He said, "NO!" A few minutes later I saw a storm drain and ran to hurl in it, breaking formation. I do not remember the punishment for this action, but it was severe.

I was told that I drink too much and to stop it. So I started to drink much less. The sickness in my stomach went away. To this day I probably do not drink enough.

We also had a PT (Physical Training) instructor or physical trainer. Once, I happened to be passing near the PT instructor and my DI who were talking together. As I was passing the PT instructor, he called me over to him. He asked me if my DI was hard on me. Immediately I knew I was in trouble. What could I answer? I needed one quickly. If I said he was easy on me, he would be harder. I needed to answer fast, so I said, "Yes Sir!"

My DI said, "I'm hard on you huh?!?! Report to me when we get back you MF-er!!!"

When we got back to the barracks, I went to his office and rapped on the door frame. The door was seldom closed. He told me to go out in the hallway and do five million side straddle hops (jumping jacks). I thought to myself, "Five million? I can't even count to five million! How the hell am I going to do them? How am I going to know when to stop? Is he serious about this? He sure looks serious! I had better start doing them..." I was in a hallway with a wooden floor. No one else was around. I was doing jumping jacks for what seemed hours. I decided to rest my arms and keep jumping. He would feel the vibration of the jumping and never know I was resting my arms. As soon as I did this (I don't know if it was coincidence or if he was watching me), as soon as I stopped moving my arms he came out of the office. He punched me, knocked me down, and gave me a kick in the ribs. I immediately stood back up to attention and he said, "Get the hell out of here!" I quickly departed and returned to standing at attention in front of my rack with the rest of the platoon. I was so tired from doing jumping jacks that I was relieved it was all over. My new motto was becoming: A little beating never really hurt anyone. I know he could have hit me much harder if he had wanted to.

I once saw a person crack in boot camp. I never saw anything like it before in my life. We were standing at attention in front of our rack for hours. Soon one of the guys on the other end of the squad bay started to scream and cry. He started to throw his gear. He was making noises I have never heard a person make before. Mucus was profusely running out of his nose, and tears were streaming down his face. The drill instructor walked in, turned around, and walked out. Just minutes later, an ambulance pulled up in front of the barracks. Three men in white coats came rushing in. They struggled with the guy, and all the while the DI was swearing at him and calling him names. They put him in a straight jacket. That was the first and only time that I ever saw a real straight jacket. You see them in movies, but never for real. They drug him away, and we never saw him again. Much later the DI told us, "He is home screwing your girlfriend right now. How do you feel about that?"

I also remember a time when we were all standing at attention in front of our racks, and a DI from another platoon walked in. We called attention and our DI said, "At ease." The DI from the other platoon told a recruit he had brought with him to get down on his knees, which he did. Then he said, "Tell these recruits what you would do to get out of the Marine Corps!"

He said with tears in his eyes, "I would suck a dick to get out of the Marine Corps, Sir!" I have no idea how many times his DI made him repeat this statement or to how many people. Our DI told us that he was rejected from the Marine Corps.

Our DI, or possibly one of the guys (I wasn't there at the time), punched someone in the face, breaking his jaw. He was taken to sick bay. The DI told us later, "It is totally up to you guys. You can say that he fell over a foot locker, or you can stay here for another three months until this issue is resolved". No one wanted to stay longer than necessary so we said he fell over a foot locker.

If you have ever been to Parris Island, South Carolina in the summer, you will find out about an insect the DI's called sand fleas (I think southerners call them chiggers). I believe the Marine Corps imported them just to make our stay more pleasant. In all my time there I never actually saw a sand flea. I have no idea what they are or what they look like. They would drive us crazy, if we were not already. They would bite us and it would hurt, but we were not allowed to move. We would be standing in formation, at attention for hours, with these little critters biting us, and we could do nothing about it. Once our DI turned his back to us, and one of the guys quickly slapped a sand flea that had been biting him. As soon as he did this, we heard a voice from another DI who was standing silently behind us. We had no idea he was there, where he came from, or how long he had been watching.

We were told to get down on our hands and knees and look in the grass to find the dead sand flea. There we were, approximately seventy five of us crawling on our hands and knees looking for a dead sand flea. I remember thinking, "How could you possibly find one in the grass?"

After about ten minutes, one of the guys said, "Sir I found it!"

"Let me see it!" The DI looked at it and said, "The one he killed was a female, this one is a male. Keep looking! And when we find it, the miserable turd who killed my sand flea will dig a hole six feet deep and give it a proper burial!"

We had to hit the rack when told to do so and lay there at attention until we fell asleep. On occasions, we would have to sing the Marine Corps hymn before we fell asleep - "From the Halls of Montezuma to the Shores of Tripoli. We will fight our country's battles on land, in air, and sea."

We were kept so busy that women seldom entered our mind at boot camp. Seldom did you have time for such luxuries as thinking about women. Remember, we were mostly eighteen year-olds - walking hormones.

One time, one of the guys snuck crackers from the mess hall into our barracks. Somehow the DI caught him. He had to crush all the crackers up in his rack and sleep through the night with them there.

Did you ever hear rumors of recruits having to clean toilets, urinals, or the wooden floors with a tooth brush? Been there, done that.

While in formation, standing at attention (which seemed like all the time), a DI would walk through the ranks inspecting our dress. If you had a pocket open, he would say, "If you didn't bother to use this button so graciously issued to you by my beloved Corps, I guess you don't need it!" He ripped it off and put it in your pocket so you would have to sew it on later. Once the DI came over to me, grabbed me by the jaw, and said, "Did you shave this morning maggot?"

I said "Yes Sir!"

He said "Well, next time use a fucking blade!" We were called nice little names by our DI. Some of their most common used were scum bag, maggot, and turd. A good name was boot. I always wondered where they got these colorful characterizations. Was it in the DI training manual? Our DI's were very well trained. They had the ability to amplify their voices twice as loud as a normal human being. They used theatrics to make us feel far worse than the situation warranted. I admired them because it seemed as if they knew everything.

One of my least favorite things to do in boot camp was learning to drill on the parade deck, hour after hour on this hot black top. It was a big, hot parking lot. We wore a plastic helmet liner that was painted silver. One DI told us it was to protect our heads - that our brain would fry without it. These liners were called chrome domes by our DI's. We carried a canteen with water, which we were only allowed to drink from when told to do so. Of course we carried an M14 rifle. I believe it weighed eight to nine pounds.

When one of us screwed up, we would have to stand on the grass at the edge of the parade deck and hold our rifle in our hands with our arms extended straight out in front of us, while everyone else resumed drills. After about five minutes, our arms would begin to shake and it would drop slightly. Then the DI would stop the rest of the platoon and give us some special attention. He would yell at us to keep our hands up and our arms straight. He would go back to drilling the platoon. Soon he would stop again and bark, "Get those fucking arms straight!" Soon he was back and hung a canteen full of water on our rifles. It was almost impossible to hold up the rifle at this point because now we had our rifle and a full canteen of water hanging on it. It would be quite painful. Finally, he would let us go back to drilling. It is amazing that we would find relief in drilling. I remember at times I would see a single cloud coming toward us. I would think "We will get shade for a few minutes. It is getting closer, very soon now." Then cloud would go around us. I saw this happen dozens of times. I thought, "How do they do it? They must get the clouds to go around this place somehow."

We would have classes on how to take our rifle apart and put it back together blind folded. I was kind of afraid I would not be able to complete this difficult task; but the Marine Corps had a system. The reason for this training was so if our rifle became disabled, we could repair it in the dark.

When one person screwed up, we all would have to pay for it. Therefore, if someone screwed up, often the guys would talk to him at night when all was quiet. If it persisted, they would hold a blanket party. Someone would grab the recipient's blanket and pull it over his head. Some other guys would punch him or hit him with a sock that had a bar of soap at the end of it. This was encouraged by the DI, but never formally. Luckily I never received or participated in a blanket party.

We finally made it to the rifle range. I was so happy! I was very used to rifles from hunting, and I was a fairly good shot. The DI told us we would have it easy now. We were made to hold the rifle in different positions for hours on end. This was painful after a while. At the end of the day, we would be standing at attention in front of our racks. The DI would walk around and ask us our score for the day. If it was too low, he would punch us in the chest, knocking us onto our rack. One day, we all did poorly so we all had to squeeze into the shower area together. It was a small area so it quickly became stuffy, and we could barely breathe. We were all sweating and hot as hell. The DI told us to get out before one of us passed out. We all had to qualify as a Marksman (okay), Sharpshooter (good), or Expert (the best). Getting an "Unqualified" was not tolerated, and there would be severe punishments. Qualifying on the range was the primary focus of our training and it was expected of everyone. Out of boot camp, I was a Sharpshooter. Later when I had to re-qualify, I shot a very high Expert using the M16. Now that was more like it! I was very proud of that accomplishment.

While we were at the range and no DI's were around, one of the rifle range instructors said to me, "You always look so unhappy. Why are you so unhappy?"

I quickly replied, "What do I have to be happy about here?" I forgot Sir at the end and braced myself for a repercussion. Either he did not catch it, or he did not care.

He immediately pointed to an American flag flying about two hundred feet away and said, "Right there is something to be very happy about". Thinking about it later, he was right. I should have been happy to be born in this country and to have the opportunity to serve it.

After the rifle range, we moved to the pistol range. This was not nearly as important as the rifle, since the M16 is the major weapon of the Marines. I was not used to hand guns, so I never finished with a very high score using the Colt .45. I shot Marksman with the hand gun which was okay because if you did not qualify, you were in a lot of trouble. After a day of shooting, the DI told three of us to put the target frames away. While doing so, I passed three pistol instructors. One called me over and he said, "Where are you from?"

I said, "Pennsylvania, Sir."

He struck me across the throat with a target frame and barked, "Where at in Pennsylvania?"

I replied, "Near Allentown, Sir."

He said, "That's better. Next time I ask you a question, be more specific. I'm from Pennsylvania, too. Now get out of here."

I went back to my platoon, and the DI came over to me. He asked, "Did that instructor hit you or harass you?"

I said, "Yes, Sir." He walked down to the three instructors with a very angry walk. They were too far away to tell what he said, but he was with them for a while. I guess other instructors were not allowed to abuse us without our DI's permission.

Soon came the obstacle course including the slide for life. This is where we slid down a cable that was attached to a high tower on one end and the ground on the other end. As we slid down the cable we were given the signal to let go; and we dropped into a mud hole. There was a high log system that we had to climb up and over. It was about twenty feet high. Then there were eight foot walls we had to climb over. We had to climb the rope ladders like the ones for boarding a ship. I actually ended up doing this once, and it is totally different than the training. Of course the ocean is never smooth, and that means that the ship you are on and the boat you are going down to do not rock in sync. One is going up and the other is going down or one is swinging away from the other and they come together with a bang. We had to watch and time it so we were not caught in the bang when we jumped into the small boat.

Then there were the pugil stick fights. Size did not matter. We put on a leather boxing helmet and were given a stick, like a broom handle, with what looked almost like a boxing glove on each end. This event was to give us practice at bayonet fighting. I fought in several matches and did okay. Soon I got paired with someone a little smaller than me. I thought to myself, "I am really going to kick this little guy's ass!" Well, to my amazement, he kicked my ass. I was kind of stunned and embarrassed. The little bastard should have more respect for someone bigger than he was! Right?

Pugil Stick Fighting

Next came combat swimming. Here we learned *drown proofing,* as the DI called it. We would have to jump off a high tower which represented a ship. We had to float for a long period of time in case we went overboard on a ship. The method was to take a deep breath and hold it, paddle with your arms once to bring you to the top, and hold your breath. Then let it out, paddle for another breath, and then repeat the process. I hated it. The Marine Corps could take something as fun as swimming or shooting and make it difficult.

When in boot camp, we were never called a Marine. We could not dress in the ways that the Marines do. We were not Marines until we finished boot camp. I remember the DI telling us, "You dumb sons of bitches volunteered for this. You have no one to blame but yourself. You have less rights and privileges than a prisoner." I used to think to myself, "How can they legally treat us like this?"

Boot camp is very hard - mentally, physically and emotionally. It is designed to weed out the people who cannot handle it, at a surprisingly large rate. The belief is that it is better to break someone in boot camp than on the battle field. Once I got to Vietnam, I was glad they had trained us the way that they did.

Infantry Training Regiment

When boot camp was finally over, we thought we had it made. Not so in good old Marine Corps fashion. We were transported to Camp Geiger, North Carolina, which is a part of Camp Lejeune. This is where we learned infantry training.

The Marine Corps believes that everyone needs to be trained as a basic grunt, or infantry man. "Every Marine is, first and foremost, a rifleman". There have been incidents throughout Marine Corps history where Marines, regardless of rank or position, were put on the front lines, including patients in hospitals. Everyone who could lift a rifle was given one and put on the lines to defend the encampment. This meant that wherever one was headed in the Corps, they needed to know how to be part of the infantry.

The good part of ITR (Infantry Training Regiment) was that we got to fire every small weapon in the USMC arsenal. The guys back home would have been so jealous! We got to throw the old pineapple grenades. I still have the pin from the first grenade I ever threw. We also got to shoot the famed BAR (Browning Automatic Rifle). I remember firing the flame thrower. I did not like that much napalm being on my back. It was a little too close for comfort. When I did fire it, I kept thinking that a freak wind might come by and blow it back on me. It was a very windy day. We fired the 3.5 inch rocket launcher, also better known as a Bazooka. That was kind of cool.

I remember firing a rifle with a grenade attachment on the front. We put a cartridge, that was crimped and had no bullet in the chamber. There was an attachment on the rifle where we could screw on a grenade launcher. Then we attached the rifle grenade. When it fired, it almost felt like it would rip our arm off. It was hard to hold the rifle when firing it. I had no idea where the grenade hit because I was too shocked by the kick of the rifle.

The worst part of ITR was the forced marches. We would walk for mile after mile with a forty pound pack, nine pound helmet, and a nine pound rifle. As we walked, we would let the guy in front get a little further ahead than the gap we were supposed to hold. We were walking in dry sand. It would get churned up from so many men walking on it. It would get soft; and the guys near the rear, like me, would sink in the sand up to our ankles with each step. It made it so much harder to walk. There were hundreds of us, one column on one side of the road and another column on the other. Soon the instructor would yell, "Close it up!"

Then all the instructors would call, "Close it up!" Soon everyone would move faster to close the gap. By the time the gap got to us near the rear of the column, we had to run like hell to close the gap. It sucked.

We could talk in ITR and even had some evenings off, which was much different than boot camp. We could go to the PX or Post Exchange and buy what we wanted. We could have a candy bar for the first time in months. At ITR, life was easier than it had been at Parris Island. We did have nice things like night obstacle courses. There was the one where we crawled on our bellies under barb wire while they shot live rounds above us. We had to watch where we crawled. There were large indentations in the ground with some small rocks around them. As I got very close to an indentation with rocks around it, I was curiously looking at it to see what it was, and then it exploded. It was made to seem like real combat. I learned later that nothing can really prepare you for live combat.

There were obstacle ropes set up about twelve feet high from one tower to another that we had to cross. One of the sections of the course had three ropes, two to hold on to and one to walk on. Some of them had only two ropes, one at the top and one at the bottom. We walked on one and held on to the one above our heads for balance. Imagine doing that at night in the pitch dark.

The Marine Corps Force Recon trained where we were located. I heard so many stories about these guys that I was afraid of them. I was gung ho when I went in to the Marines, but these guys were too much! I heard stories where they dropped them off on an island with a knife and poncho and came back for them weeks later. Sometimes they dropped them off in the ocean, miles from shore with a pack, a rifle, and a helmet; and they made their own way back. Their missions usually entailed having to jump out of a plane behind enemy lines, retrieve certain information about the enemy, and then find their own way back. When I was in Vietnam, the Recon unit had a board with their names on it. They hung human ears by wire under their names to show how many kills they had.

The Force Recon would have to climb a high water tower near our location and do pull ups off the side of it in the middle of the night. They would go for twenty mile runs at night. They would hide in swamps; and if their instructor saw them, he would jump on them. Most of them were certified scuba divers and were jump qualified (parachutist).

There were steam pipes (running along the road about ten feet above the ground) that fed heat to all the barracks. Sometimes we would hear a weird noise because these guys were running on top of them at night.

On one operation in the Mediterranean, we had a small fire going at night. There were two guards walking around the tanks while the rest of us gathered around the fire telling stories. A lieutenant walked into our group. He said, "Did anyone see anyone go through this area?"

We all said, "No!" He said his whole platoon of Force Recon went through our area. He said they went inside the tanks and wrote down serial numbers of some of the equipment to verify they were there. Not one of us knew it. My respect and fear of them increased.

The one story that really stood out in my mind at ITR was the one about a guy who took out a fifty dollar bill. He said to me, "If I hold this on your arm and burn a hole through it with a cigarette, I will give it to you." Being the dummy I was, I had to try it. I was determined to do it. It was now a test of manhood. I would do it no matter what the cost. I would show the guys how brave I was - more like how really **stupid**.

After about five minutes of enduring pain with the cigarette almost burnt down, he said, "Well it is quite obvious it will not burn a hole in the fifty."

I said "Yeah, I guess so". So he took it away. All the guys were gathered around and wanted to see the mark. It was a nasty big red one. The next day it was huge and sore. A scab formed over it, but it got infected under the scab. I would squeeze it and all kinds of puss would come out. I could not go to my instructor and say I burned myself. I would get in big trouble if they found out how. I did not know what to do, but I knew I had to do something. This went on for about a week and it grew to about two and a half inches in diameter. I got the bright idea to pull off the scab and put aftershave lotion on it. I knew aftershave had some alcohol in it. It hurt like hell, but I did it every day for several weeks. Soon it started to get a scab with nothing under it. I hid the wound the whole time. I still have the scar, and he had the fifty. By the way, do not try this at home.

When we were finished with our training, we were called to formation and given our orders. My orders said Second Tank Battalion which was very close to where we were. I was told to jump in the back of a truck with a canvas cover over it. I threw my sea bag over the tailgate. As it landed inside, I was surprised to see another sea bag follow it. I had not seen anyone near me.

I climbed in, and the owner of the other sea bag followed. We were sitting on our sea bags in the back against the tailgate. Sitting inside were three Marines leaning against the back of the cab. They were all staring at us. I felt very uncomfortable. We had just finished our training, and I did not know what to expect. Everyone in the world was superior to us.

Two of the Marines wore rank insignia, and one did not. The one that did not was much larger than all of us. I knew he was not a new guy because his uniform was well worn and faded, but he was a private just like me.

He stared at me. I was getting very uncomfortable. What was his problem? I sure did not want any trouble already. As we rode along he kept looking at me. I did not want any problem so I did not look at him or any of the others. They were all sitting facing the back. The other new guy and I were facing front. I felt like hockey players at a face off.

Although I did not look at him I could feel his stare. Finally, still staring at me, he said, "Are you a tough guy?" I did not know what to think. Who would the rest of the guys support, a new private or one that had been in the Marines for a while?

I said, "No!"

He said, "Good, 'cause I don't like tough guys!" I quickly looked away from his stare.

After a few minutes he said, "Are you sure you are not a tough guy, cause you look like one to me!"

I said, "No!' That was all that was said on the whole half hour trip.

I later found out the guy in the back of the truck who kept staring at me was busted down to private many times. If someone asked him to do something, he would do it. If someone demanded he do something, he got very belligerent. I learned then that it is much easier to ask someone to do something rather than demand it. If asking did not work, then I demanded. It was something that I always remembered.

When we arrived at the Company Headquarters, we were escorted in to the First Sergeant's office. The other guy from infantry training and I stood at attention in front of his desk. He said, "At ease." We stood in the at ease position (at attention with arms behind your back, somewhat less rigid).

He said, "Which one of you is Private Hoch?"

I said, "I am Sir!"

He said, "Don't call me sir; I'm not a dammed officer. You guys are both to go on thirty days leave. Make sure you are back on time. Now get out of here."

We got a cab to the bus station. The other guy wanted to strike up a conversation saying, "Where are you headed?" I sure did not want to miss my bus, so I kind of blew him off.

Little did I know then the other guy was Al, and I would spend more time with him than anyone else while I was in the Marines.

Wow, home again. I survived it all. I was now a Marine and very proud of it. When I got home, I did what the others had done before me and became a member of an elite group of warriors. I told all of the younger kids how great it was to be a Marine. I told them that through all the training the Corps tears you down to where you feel like you are the lowest form of life on earth. Then, slowly, they build your confidence to where you are very proud of your accomplishments. At eighteen, becoming a Marine is a huge success. I felt like I could do anything! I think that is why the military wants people so young.

The Med Cruises

After my thirty day leave, I arrived at Camp Lejeune in North Carolina. I was told that we were going on a Med Cruise. Sounded fun to me! "What the hell is a Med cruise?", I asked the guys on the tank. The U. S. has a fleet of ships and a battalion of Marines in the Mediterranean Sea at all times to protect embassies and civilian populace in times of an emergency.

That cruise was my first real experience with poverty outside of the United States. Poverty in the states does not really compare to seeing it in other parts of the world. A garbage barge came next to the ship, and our ship unloaded its garbage. Some of the workers on the barge started to eat some of the best looking leftover food – now **that** is poverty. How hungry would you have to be to do that?

Now we were a tank platoon, so you may ask (as I did), "How do you get a tank on a ship?"

"You will see", is the answer I received. Now, I am not quite sure how I ended up on the tanks, not that I was upset about it. One of the other guys asked when we would go to school to learn about the tanks, which is a fairly complicated piece of equipment. The reply was that it is on the job training.

Most of the time, when you are a new guy in tanks, you are assigned to a loader's position, which is as it sounds, you load the main gun. The progression in tanks is loader, driver, gunner, tank commander, light section leader, heavy section leader, platoon sergeant and platoon commander. The light section is made up of two tanks. The heavy section was made up of three tanks. A tank platoon is made up of five tanks. There are four platoons to a company. One is headquarters platoon, which includes maintenance, flame tanks, and a blade tank (a tank with a huge blade like that on a bull dozer). I was made a driver from the beginning, for some reason that was unknown to me.

Wow! I was a tank driver. I felt like I was really cool. I was already a driver. I skipped over the job as loader. The three other guys who came to the Tank Battalion when I did were all loaders.

I was put on a tank that had an old Gunnery Sergeant as the

commander. He was also our Platoon Sergeant. He had twenty two years in the Marine Corps. He was cocky and sure of himself. Our Platoon Commander was a new Second Lieutenant. He was very new to the Marine Corps, just like me.

One day we were on maneuvers, and we stopped for a while. Everyone left the tank except for me. I was sitting in the driver's compartment with the engine running, waiting for someone to tell me what to do. Soon, both the Platoon Commander and the Gunny climbed into the turret. They had someone come in and take out the breach block on the main gun. This was part of our normal PM, preventative maintenance. The breach block was a very heavy piece of steel that dropped down in place after a round was loaded into the main gun. It had the firing pin inside of it.

One of the guys in our platoon once used a rope instead of a chain hoist to remove the breach block. As he was removing the breach block, he put his finger in the hole to remove the firing pin and the rope slipped. The breach block cut his finger off. They sewed it back on; but it never took, and he was discharged from the Marines because it was his trigger finger.

Anyway, as I sat in the driver compartment I shut the engine off. The Gunny and the Lieutenant started to talk about how to bore sight the main gun, which is to make the main gun and the sights line up. Soon their conversation became heated. They started yelling at each other in loud, angry tones. I was the only other person in the tank. I tried to make myself as small and inconspicuous as possible. I was as quiet as a mouse. They did not like each other very much.

One day on maneuvers the Gunny jumped into the tank and said over the intercom that we were going to race the Lieutenant, and we were going to win. We lined up and the Gunny said, "Go!" to me on the intercom. I floored the pedal. We were only going at half speed. I was trying to think of what the hell I was doing wrong. I was dumbfounded. We were losing the race. I could have **run** faster than we were going.

When we finally got to the finish line the Gunny came down on the fender to the driver compartment and called me all kinds of names for quite some time. Finally, after the cheery pep talk, a curious maintenance man came over and opened the engine plate. He found a linkage arm that had become disconnected. He put it back on and the tank went the speed it was supposed to go.

The Gunny never said, "I should not have gone off on you like that" or "Sorry. It wasn't your fault." Much later he **did say** that if he were going into combat, he would like to have me on his tank. He said, "You never get rattled."

We drove the tanks to a railroad loading station on base. I did not have much experience driving the tank at this point. There was a very steep concrete ramp with a railroad flat car in front of it. A ground guide lined me up to drive the tank up the ramp. He told me to go straight ahead. As I drove forward I could not see the ground at all. It was a very scary feeling. The tank tracks hung over the flat cars by some eight inches on either side. I was very high in the air and could see nothing but sky. I kept creeping forward until the front end came crashing down on the flat car. There was not much room for error and having recently gotten out of boot camp and ITR, I knew what would happen had I screwed up. Besides getting my ass chewed out by my superiors, I knew I would never live it down with my peers.

The flat bed train cars with the tanks and guards (which was my position at the time) were taken to Morehead City, North Carolina to be unloaded on a beach. We sat there for days waiting for the ships. At times while guarding the tanks someone would sneak into town and get a six pack of beer. We rotated as guards, and I was sent back to Battalion headquarters. We got word a few days later that some of the guards were driving a tank around while intoxicated and drove over a jeep and trailer, both loaded for the cruise. They were crushed with all the gear in them. They were both useless. Charges were brought up on both guards. One of them deserted rather than spend time in the brig. The other blamed the deserter and was given a less severe punishment. I was happy I was not involved.

Soon the whole platoon arrived at the beach to camp and wait. Finally, the ships of the fleet arrived. The ship we were going on was an LSD, or landing ship dock. It was named the USS Casa Grande. It was probably a half mile from the beach. It had a huge tailgate in the back (or aft) which opened like a pick up truck's tailgate. The ship was flooded with water. Small boats called Mike boats (landing craft personnel carrier) and U-boats (landing craft utility boats) came off the ship and headed for the beach. They drove right up on the beach. They had a tail gate in the front. The two Mike boats each held one tank. The bigger U boats held three tanks. We backed the tanks onto the boats and the ramps closed. The boats backed up with powerful engines and drove right into the back of the ship with us and the tanks on board. The tail gate was raised and the water pumped out. The tanks were chained to the boats, the boats were chained to the ship, and away we went for the Mediterranean.

An Ontose coming off of a Mike boat and
tanks getting ready to come off of a U boat

A few days after we shipped out, we hit a typhoon. This was my first time on the ocean, and I was very unhappy with the whole situation. I had sea sickness from the very first day. My superiors decided that I should be sent to serve mess duty on the ship. I was so sick I could not do anything so I was taken off of mess duty to suffer in my rack. Sea sickness is one hell of an ailment. I felt like I was dying. I do not think I would have cared if I did die at that point. The ship was rocking so badly that I could stand on one side of the ship, and looking straight down across the deck, see the ocean on the other side. I saw one of the ships in the fleet get the whole front end covered by a huge wave. The ship was a troop carrier and was twice the size of ours. I remember thinking while this was all happening that I hope to hell the Navy knew what they were doing. It did not help that I had always had a fear of deep, dark water and there was no shortage of that!

Our compartment was like a long, high, narrow hallway. It had racks on both sides. The racks, or small, flat mattresses (like a cot), were canvas with rope webbing around the edges. They looked so primitive for that day and age. They were stacked approximately eight racks high, and you had just enough room to roll over - barely brushing the canvas above you. I learned quickly that it was best to be high in the racks for two reasons. First, if you were near the top, you were less likely to be stepped on as one climbed to the upper racks. Second, and most important, if someone got sick from being sea sick or from drinking too much on shore leave, you were safer near the top. The only problem was that you had to climb really high to get to the top racks. You ended up stepping on others as you climbed to your bunk, which pissed people off. Our compartment was below the water line. I just did not like this big piece of steel called a ship floating around like a cork in the huge, rough ocean. Many mornings we would have to search for our foot lockers, which were stored on the deck below our racks, and ended up getting scattered around from the rough ocean.

Once my sickness subsided (which felt like a lifetime), I would go out on deck to see if I could see anything besides water. I was mobile, but I still felt queasy. After a few days the fleet separated. All of the ships spread out so we could not see any of them anymore. It was like we were on a huge round piece of blue paper with nothing else around us for days, which soon became weeks. Once, while standing on the bow (front) of the ship, a little bird landed on the deck near a few of us Marines. It was all out of breath and panting frantically. He must have flown some distance and was too tired to continue. I thought about trying to give it some water. One of the guys walked over to it, looked at it for a while, than stepped on it and crushed it and kicked it into the ocean. I was so pissed at him for killing it after it worked so hard to find a resting place. It finally made it to safety only to be killed by some idiot. Some mornings we found dead flying fish on the deck but usually nothing else. This was my first time at sea, or on a ship, so everything was exciting to me. Had it not been for the sea sickness, it would have been awesome.

If I remember correctly, it took us twenty one days to cross. We arrived in Rota, Spain which was a Spanish base. We were not allowed off of base. There was not much to do, so we hung around the ship. After some time, we arrived in Naples, Italy and were granted shore leave.

My friends and I decided to do what Marines do when they are on leave - we drank. I was drinking with some friends in a very large, crowded bar when a young lady sat beside me. I had a very hard time understanding her, as her English was very broken; but there was no mistaking what she wanted when she started to rub me in places that embarrassed the hell out of me. It was a great place for an eighteen or nineteen year old kid, with all of the alcohol you could drink and all of the women you could pay for. They were cheap and very pretty. I was no virgin, but this was unbelievable!

On one Med cruise, we landed in Crete with the tanks. There was a very high hill near us. Once we got settled in, one of the Sergeants came up to Al and me. He told us to take a radio and a 30 caliber machine gun with a tripod and go up on top of the hill for FO's (Forward Observers). We were like the lookouts. If we saw the enemy we would let the platoon know so that they could prepare.

Al said, "Take plenty of smokes. It will be a long day up there."

We asked if we would get relief in a few hours. The answer was, "No. You are up there until we tell you to come down". Up we went. It was a long and hard journey. It was about a mile up a very steep hill. When we finally got to the top, we were wet with sweat. We took our shirts off so we only had our tee shirts on. There was an indentation in the ground which made a perfect fox hole, so we used it and settled in.

I was really starting to like this duty. We were by ourselves, no one telling us what to do. It was a very nice, sunny day. What a life. Soon a shepherd came by with some sheep. He looked at us and kept walking at a fast pace. Al held up a pack of smokes. The guy glanced at us and walked on like he didn't give a shit that we were there. I said, "What the hell was that for?"

He replied, "You never know." I forgot about the incident. About an hour later the shepherd came back with gallons of home-made wine in leather vessels. Even the vessels were homemade. We gave him two packs of smokes, and he gave us all the wine. American cigarettes were like gold over there. It got so much better. We were sitting up there in the sun with smokes and wine. How could you not love the good old USMC for this one?

We were up there for a good eight hours or so. When we were called back, we dumped the water from our canteens and filled them with wine and left the leather vessels behind. As we came down the hill, one of the guys kept watching us. Soon the whole platoon came over as we fell and staggered down the hill. Most were laughing at us, but our superiors were pretty pissed. They told us to dump out our canteens. That was when they saw the wine. They said, "You idiots could get a poisoning from the aluminum in the canteens and the wine combined." We got a good ten minute lecture for that one. I always expected a later punishment - guard duty for a week or something like that - but it never came. Everyone wondered how we had gotten wine on the mountain, but we were not about to give away our secret.

A few weeks later, we landed on Malta which is an island in the Mediterranean. It was the most frequently bombed island in WW2 because everyone wanted it for a base. I enjoyed it there. I liked the island. It was always sunny and bright. All of the women always wore dresses and never slacks. They even wore dresses when they were working in the fields. That is the only country I ever remember being like that. The British had bases there, and they were pulling out at the islanders' request. The U. S. was moving in to the bases as they were moving out. It was one of the few areas where the people actually liked Americans.

We were not allowed to take the tanks on the island so we

had to act as grunts. Backpacks, helmets, and rifles were issued but not ammo. There was no need for ammo. It was just a war game. On the ride in (we rode in on small mike boats) I tried to imagine what it must have been like in WW2 on the D-day landings or the Pacific landings. You could never imagine what it was like unless you lived it. I know that from experience. People asked me, "What was it like in Vietnam?" or, "What does it feel like to kill someone?" How can you possibly give an answer to a question like that?

Although we were confined to the base, we had plenty of beer. I started to talk to a British soldier. I asked him if there was a town around here with any women. By this time, I had been in the service for six months and felt like an old salt. He told me that there was one about ten miles up the road, and there were plenty of women there, since no one is allowed off the base. As we sat drinking, I started to think about our situation. Finally I said, "We should wait until dark, sneak out under the concertina wire (like barbed wire but it has more strands and it is curled) and go to town". To my amazement most of the guys agreed.

When it got dark, someone said to me, "What's the plan?" By this time, I had realized it was probably a bad idea, but I couldn't back out now.

We looked for a spot to sneak out and found one. Soon six of us were walking up a very dark, windy road. After about a mile we saw a jeep coming and knew it must be an officer. Four of us hid in the brush on the side of the road. The other two (one of which was Al) jumped over a stone fence about two feet high on the other side of the road. After the jeep was well down the road, I called to Al. No answer. I walked to the stone fence expecting him to stand up at any minute. I looked down over the fence into the dark and called again. He finally answered. I said, "Where are you"?

He said, "Down here!" It was so dark all I could see was blackness. Apparently, there was about a twenty foot drop on the other side of the stone fence. I stood there laughing so hard, as they made their way back up the very steep hill by pulling themselves up with small trees.

The walk into town took much longer than expected, and some of the guys started complaining. One of them said to me, "I thought you said it was ten miles? We must have gone more than that so far!" I defended myself by saying that is what the British soldier said.

We were almost sober by the time we walked into town, but we made up for it after we arrived. There were girls all over the place, and they were cheap, too. We actually met one girl from California who was there trying to make extra money for school. We were there for hours, having a great time, when for some reason, someone punched a stained glass door.

We all ran out and looked around. We spotted a taxi. We ran over to it, but by the time we got in, the police arrived and blocked the taxi in. I tried the best that I could to shut every one up and let one person do the talking. I should have saved my breath. Everyone was yelling. It was quite a commotion. Soon the police said we could go. We were all very surprised and happy.

At this point, there was no way I could have found the way back on my own. There was so much confusion on how to get back and, before you knew it, the taxi dropped us off right in front of the barracks. We snuck in, trying to be as quiet as possible. It must have been at least four o'clock in the morning when we got back. At five o'clock in the morning we were awakened and sent to mess. I could not eat. We were told to get our pack, helmet, and rifle and meet in formation.

We went on a twenty mile force march, which means we did not stop at all. It was so hot, and there were many hills. I thought I was going to die. I could think of nothing but drinking a gallon of water and sacking out in a rack. It was horrible! Some of the tankers did drop out and rode back in a truck. In my severe pain and misery, it did cross my mind that I had not seen Al so far. I wondered what had happened to him. My water was gone in the first hour. I was determined to finish the march, and I did.

When we finally got back, Al was there to greet us, laughing his heart out. I said, "Where the hell were you?"

He said, "I think I broke my ankle and had to sit it out. I told the Corpsman that I fell getting out of the top rack when I got up." The Corpsman said that there may be a small break, but he would be okay in a week or so. If not, come back to see him then.

I asked, "What the hell did you do all day?"

He replied, "Lay in my rack." I couldn't say anything, so I just walked away. Why the hell didn't I think of doing something like that?

Was it all worth it? NO! I wondered if the police let us go because they knew our commanding officers would do worse to us than they could.

On another occasion, Al, a few others, and I went to a nice bar on Malta. We did not have to sneak into town this time so we were in full uniform. We got a large table in this very crowded bar and started to drink and have fun. Soon, Al spotted this very cute girl and asked her to dance. She was wearing a beige suit top, a beige skirt, a white blouse, and a red scarf. She was about five foot, eight inches tall - a really pretty brunette with shoulder length hair.

As they were dancing she got warm and removed her jacket. Al removed his jacket. She removed her red scarf. Al removed his tie. She removed her blouse, Al his shirt. Soon she was dancing in her bra and panties and Al in his Marine Corps issued boxers. Everyone in the bar was laughing hysterically. That was Al. He did all kinds of stupid shit like that. We had such a great time that night. I am sure the bar pulled in lots of money with us there. I do not think I have ever been anywhere where everyone had such a good time.

I once heard that Al, on his third Med cruise, was intoxicated on the ship in the middle of the Atlantic Ocean, trying to drop the anchor because he wanted to go home. Naval regulations prevent anyone from having alcohol on the ships.

He came to visit me in Vietnam, and we spent some time together there. He contacted me twice after we got out of the service. Once he called at about two o'clock in the morning. He was supposed to meet a bunch of us in Las Vegas. He never showed up in Vegas. He stopped all communications and that was the last I had any contact with him. I would really like to talk to him again.

On the next Med cruise, we were preparing to go on a landing. The ocean was rough, and the tanks were wet from the ocean mist. I climbed up the side of the turret to go inside the hatch. I slipped and hit my knee very hard on the side of the turret. It was extremely painful. I stood up and passed out. The next thing I knew, I was lying on the steel deck of the ship with one of the guys staring me in the face. They carried me up to sick bay on a stretcher and put me in a rack.

Meanwhile the rest of the platoon went on to the landing. I laid there in sick bay for quite some time. The Chief Petty Officer, who was the Corpsman, sat in his chair drinking coffee. I had a cut on the back of my head from the fall and pieces of grit from the steel deck embedded in my head around the wound. My back hurt like hell. I laid there for quite some time. The Corpsman never got out of his chair to look at me. He said, "Whenever you feel better, you can leave." I felt stupid just lying there, so I figured if he was not even going to look at me, I should just go. I got on a small Mike boat going into shore and caught up to the rest of my platoon. That night they put me on guard duty, and my back was killing me. I had back problems for years after that.

By this time, I was a Corporal and Tank Commander. We had a big operation where we were to make a mock beach assault landing for a group of Admirals, Generals, and Heads of State from a bunch of different countries like Italy and France. It was to be a small, mock-war type landing. We would have a little war game on the beaches as they sat in the bleachers and watched us. The tanks can handle water up to eight feet deep, if they have a fording kit, which is a system that hooks up to the exhaust and prevents water from coming in the exhaust and air cleaners.

I knew that sometimes the mike boats or U boats would hit a sand bar and could go no farther, even though the water was much deeper on the other side of the sand bar. I told my driver through the intercom that when the ramp of the mike boat drops to release the tank, floor the tank and keep it floored until we were on dry land. The high revs of the powerful tank diesel also kept water out of the rest of the system.

Our superiors wanted to make a good impression for their superiors and told us so. Here we were, five tanks and a company of grunts, ready for war. Naturally, we hit a sand bar and were quite some distance from the beach. As the ramp dropped, I told the driver to "floor it". He sat there doing nothing. As a Tank Commander, you cannot see the driver up front and under the turret. Again, I said into the intercom to "floor it." Again, nothing. The other tanks were all on the move and there we sat. I finally yelled into the intercom, "Will you get this God damned thing moving!" Finally we were off and running last for the beach. I was pissed off that we were so far behind the other tanks which were all lined up in a row and already close to shore.

When the games were finally over I walked down the fender and asked, "What happened out there?"

He replied, "I couldn't get the damn hatch closed!" He said he finally gave up on it and decided to try it without closing the hatch. He said, "I thought I was going to drown because there was so much water pouring in." I had to laugh at the thought of him submerged, driving this tank towards the beach with water pouring in. He looked like he was scared to death, even afterwards. I felt bad for yelling at him for the incident.

Back at Camp Lejeune

After the first Med cruise, I went back to Camp Lejeune. There was a Private First Class in my outfit. I was a Private. He would take great pleasure in picking on me. He was fond of saying, "Private Hoch! Front and center!" He harassed me for months. I once heard him say that he was going to "go over and cave Private Hoch's chest in". As he approached, I was lying on my rack with my feet on the floor (no boots on the rack). As he reached to grab me, I took both feet and kicked him square in the chest. He fell into the wall lockers, stood up, and walked away.

He was soon sent to the Nam, so my problems were over. I saw him again about a year later when he returned from Vietnam. He was a Corporal and I was a Sergeant. I was so very happy to see the look on his face when he realized that I was a Sergeant. It was one of my finer moments in the Marine Corps.

After my second Med cruise, I was getting much more comfortable as a Corporal and a tank commander. I felt that being a Corporal was my limit, and I would never go any higher. Sergeant was the next step, but being a Sergeant meant you had to know everything, and I knew very little. Everything was going smoothly when I was told to report to the second tank battalion commander who was a Colonel.

I kept asking myself, "What did I do wrong now?" He told me that I was being sent on temporary additional duty, or TAD. Why was it always me who got these assignments?

I was going to be temporarily attached to brig duty. I gathered up my belongings and headed to the brig guard/MP (military police) barracks. Once there, I was told I was going to be a chaser, which meant when a prisoner had to go to medical or dental I was to take him. He would be handcuffed, and I would walk behind him. I was fully responsible for him. The duty that I hated the most was searching prisoners when they came from the mess hall. We would have to do a very thorough search by feeling every place they could hide a knife. I hated this duty, but some of the prisoners seemed to enjoy it. After a week or so I was assigned prisoner exercise duty to make sure they did their exercise. Soon, I was put in a wing. The wings had a large group cell, probably seventy five prisoners to a cell much like the barracks. There was a large hallway which was the same length as the barracks. I stayed in the hallway at night while the prisoners slept. I had a key to the barracks and did go in with them every once in a while to quiet them down. Thinking about it later, it was a stupid thing to do. There was a large barred gate locking in the whole wing. There was a turnkey in a small cell like cage in between the two wings. The only way the wing bars would open was a switch in the turnkey's cell.

Not long after I was on brig duty, I was told to report to the commanding officer of the brig/MP. I think he was called the Provost Marshall. Again I was wondering what I did wrong. He only told me to report to my battalion commander back at second tanks.

I hiked over to second tanks and reported to the First Sergeant who sent me in to see the battalion commander. He asked me, "Do you know why you are here?"

I replied, "No Sir." A hundred different scenarios went through my mind.

I have had some bad reports about you. You know what we are going to do about it?"

I answered, "No sir."

He said, "We are going to promote you to Sergeant. Congratulations." Some of the guys came in to congratulate me. I was kind of dumbfounded. I wondered to myself if they had any clue as to what the hell they were doing. I didn't feel like I was a good Corporal. How the hell was I going to be a good Sergeant? I didn't know if I could do this. I went to the PX or Post Exchange and bought Sergeant chevrons, took them to a cleaner, and had them sewn onto my uniform.

When I was promoted to Sergeant, I was kind of in awe. After all, it is a General that comes up with this great plan for a mission. He asks his staff what they think. They say, "It's great", mostly because no one wants to piss off a General. He is the one who sends orders to his Colonels (who are Battalion Commanders), they pass it along to their Captains (who are Company Commanders), who pass it to their Lieutenants (who are Platoon Commanders), who pass it along to the Sergeants, who try to convince the men doing the mission that it is a worthwhile mission to risk their lives for. The Sergeant gets the men to do the mission. The General is congratulated for a small amount of American's loss of life. The men doing the mission grieve for their lost comrade in arms, whom they knew very well. After all, they slept next to each other. The General has a fine dinner, brandy, and cigars with his staff. The men eat cold C rations if the enemy is too close, sleep on the ground, and can't smoke a cigarette.

All who served in the military have their complaints. I certainly did. The officers suck, I hate this place, etc. But if you look at the larger scale: How many organizations could have that many men and women, feed them, care for them medically, and send them into horrendous conditions to risk their lives? Logistically it is a huge task - the training, the supplies, etc. It goes on and on.

Anyhow, back to the brig I went. There were red lines and yellow lines painted on the floor. A yellow line meant the prisoners had to ask permission from a guard to cross. A red line meant they were not permitted to cross. If a prisoner was walking behind you, he would have to ask permission to pass you. I would sometimes talk to some of the prisoners. I remember one conversation. The prisoner seemed like a pretty good guy. I asked him, "How long have you been in here?" He told me he had been there for seven years. I questioned, "Seven years? How long did you enlist for?"

He answered, "Three years". I asked him why he had been there for so long. He said that when they let him out, he runs away. When they bring him back, he has to make up the time he was gone plus his regular military time.

I said, "Wouldn't it make sense to just do your time and get the hell out of here?"

He mumbled, "Yeah, I guess so."

We had a duty that went something like eight hours on and twelve hours off, where we had to be available in case of an emergency. We never did have an emergency. Once I spent my eight hours on and had the weekend off. I decided to go home for the weekend. When I got back, one of the guys said to me, "You are in big trouble. We had a surprise inspection right after you left." All kinds of things raced through my mind. Well, goodbye Sergeant! I quickly went back to my Company Commander in tanks. I asked, "Sir, I have been on brig duty for some time. Can I come back now?"

He said, "Yes!" I ran back, gathered up my gear, and got out of there. I never heard anything about it. I was lucky, although for months afterward, I kept waiting for the repercussions to catch up with me.

Soon I was settled in back at the second tank battalion Sergeant's headquarters. The barracks were an H shape with a story on top. The Sergeants quarters were located in the middle of the H. It was a nice location, as it was centered for all the squad bays.

The guys were always playing jokes on each other like taking shaving cream and putting it on the hand of a sleeping person. Then, they tickled their face and watched them swat themselves with shaving lather, or they would fill someone's boots with shaving cream. Sometimes they would tie boot laces together while someone was napping, then startle them awake. The results were usually pretty amusing. Another favorite was to wet one's finger and rub the wet finger in a sleeping person's ear. It felt like a real tongue when asleep, and most of the time one would be quite aroused upon awaking.

One night, I was sleeping on my right side facing the wall. I felt someone tonguing my ear. With the absence of females, I knew it had to be one of the guys playing a joke on me. I felt that I would set an example and let them know to leave me alone. With one swift movement that would have made a professional boxer proud, I rolled over and punched at the same time. When my eyes focused, I saw a young woman lying on the floor holding her face. I felt terrible. Had I known, there would have been a total opposite reaction! I jumped out of my rack and tried to apologize, but she wanted nothing to do with me. She would not even speak to me. One of the guys got her a towel to put on her mouth because she was bleeding. I did nothing but search for women; and when they came to me, I reacted like this! During the night, one of the Sergeants had been out drinking and persuaded two young women to visit the Sergeant's quarters. They had to sneak in past the guards.

Neither of the women would have anything to do with me after that. Shortly after the incident, they left.

As can be expected, I had more than my share of harassment from the incident. The next day I heard, "We bring you some women, and you punch them? Don't you know what to do with women?" One comment was, "You mess with the bull, you get the horns."

Things were going pretty well. I was quite happy in the good ol' Marine Corps when I was called into the commander's office again. What now?? While I stood at ease in front of his desk, he stated, "We are going to send you to try out for the drill team at 8th and I in Washington."

I thought to myself, "What the hell is 8th and I? I am a tanker not a drill person. That is for grunts. Why me?!"

I packed up my belongings and caught a military prop plane to D.C. It was a cargo plane and had few seats. When I got there, I found out that the Marines have a drill team at Eight and I Street, which is called the Marine Barracks because it is where the Commandant of the Marine Corps lives. It was a nice base - very well kept.

When I went to the mess hall, I was shocked when the cook asked me what I wanted. I did not know what to say! I was never asked this question at a mess hall before. The guys there were all about the same height, same as me. They were all spit and polish. I had never seen Marines as "squared away", as we say in the Marines. I was told that they would put on a ceremony on Friday evening at the parade grounds, as they do every Friday evening. The parade grounds were a large flat, immaculately mowed lawn. A large crowd of civilians and military personnel filled the bleachers. Soon a platoon of Marines in dress blues marched out onto the grounds, followed by another. There was not a command given. This was the famous Silent Drill Team. They were, it seemed to me, in perfect harmony as they marched. They all turned in harmony and all stopped in harmony, as if they were all one organism.

One of the Marines in the ranks spun his rifle with a bayonet in circles very rapidly. He then threw it in the air about eight feet. The Marine in the rear caught it and did a mock inspection, spun it in circles, and threw it in the air again. The Marine, who originally threw it, caught it again. All this was done in complete silence. Soon, they all turned and marched off the field - all so very precise. They were so uniform, and a single command was never given.

In my two and a half years in the Marines I had never heard of these guys. I was more impressed with them than anything I had seen so far! I was to try out for this team? I am not a spit and polish person, and, these guys seemed perfect in their speech, thought, and dress. I would never fit in.

While talking to one of them I asked, "How long does it take to get ready for the ceremony?"

He stated, "About four hours." The shoes, the uniform, all of it had to be perfect and lint free. Even the buttons had to be perfect. They actually had a top and bottom that had to be aligned perfectly.

I said, "This isn't for me."

He told me that I would be interviewed by a Captain. "He is a gung ho Captain, so tell him you would rather go to the Nam than to stay here."

When I talked to him I said, "Sir, I joined the Marines to go to Vietnam and fight for my country." So I went back to Camp Lejeune.

I was in the Marines for almost three years now and did not go to the Nam. Would I survive four years and never go? Wow, that would be rare. I started thinking that maybe it wasn't so bad, and I was lucky. Well, of course that is when I got my orders.

No matter what you may think about the Vietnam War or the Vietnam Veterans who served there, my reason for going there was absolutely for the people of the United States and no other.

Second Day in Vietnam

It was February the twenty fifth of 1968. I sat on top of the tank turret soaking up the country side. It was late afternoon, peaceful and quiet. There were no people in my view, but there were plenty of trees, grass, and shrubs of various types - all new to me. Even the smell of the country was so very new. Everything was tropical. There was a musty, jungle smell in the air. The heat was diminishing, but the very high humidity was still there. This was not anything like the winters at home. Although it was humid, it was an odd humidity, as if the sun burned off the humidity as soon as it rose from the ground. Our tank was on a very high, steep hill overlooking a wide, slow running river. On the other side of the river was a dense jungle. It was late afternoon. I thought about what a pretty country it was. I thought about what had brought me here...

I had voluntarily enlisted in the US Marine Corps in March of 1965, three months before my high school graduation. I volunteered to go to Vietnam. I felt it was my duty, and the duty of every American male, to defend our country and the freedom it provides. If I had my way, every male would spend at least two years in the military serving the country. I thought about our ancestors and how they suffered for the freedom that we have today. I thought about the criminal in front of a judge getting a fair trial. I thought about the smile of the little girl down the street where I used to live. Even the post man delivering the mail had a smile. These memorable gifts all needed to be protected and preserved for future generations. I traded my home life for a Spartan's life of C rations, sleeping out in the rain, living life with very little necessities, living with people I never met before, and of course, the constant threat of enemy attack.

On the flight from Okinawa to Vietnam, I was seated next to a Staff Sergeant. Naturally the conversation on the long flight was about home and our future in combat. I had no idea what to expect when the plane landed. Would they toss me a rifle and would I run for a fox hole? We were on a civilian passenger jet complete with a phantom jet escort as we neared Vietnam. I could not see our country risking the lives of civilians, so I thought I would be safe getting off the plane at least. It couldn't be too bad, could it? I knew a sniper had killed someone getting off of the plane the week before. Wonder filled my mind, but I couldn't ask because I did not want to seem stupid or scared. After all, I was a Sergeant and was supposed to know everything.

When we finally landed, a large truck picked us up at the Da Nang airport and took us all to a transit area. We spent the night in a large barracks. Hundreds of us all packed on cots in a huge room. We did not have any blankets or pillows. We slept right on the cots in our underwear. We were not issued any weapons yet. I was with more people than I had ever met in my life, and I did not know anyone. It was my first night in Vietnam.

The first thing that I noticed about the area was the heat, heat, and more heat. Coming from the February winter at home, the heat felt even more unbearable.

The next morning was spent getting paperwork sorted out. In the afternoon I was told to wait where I was, and a jeep would pick me up to take me to battalion headquarters. So many jeeps stopped to pick up Marines that I got tired of asking, "First Tanks?" Finally a jeep pulled up, and the driver said, "First Tanks." I threw all of my possessions (a sea bag) in the back of the jeep and jumped in. On the ride to headquarters, we passed through parts of Da Nang. As far as I could see, there was poverty and destroyed buildings from rocket attacks. I was surprised to see that one building had a Coca-Cola emblem on the side of it. No English letters but I knew it was Coke. Some logos can be recognized anywhere.

One thing I will never forget about Vietnam was the poverty. I had seen poverty before but nothing like the poverty in Vietnam. When we think of poverty in America, we think of people on welfare that may not always have heat or food. In Vietnam, some of the people literally had nothing but the clothing that they wore. These people did not go to a local food shelter. They scavenged for food in the jungle. Some of them were poor rice farmers. Some were fisherman. The more fortunate ones could sell their ware at market. Some of them would take car tires and make sandals out of them to sell. We called them Ho Chi Min's. They would also take beer cans, slit them, flatten them out, shine the inside of the can, and sell them as mirrors. They used beer cans to patch roofs and to make grenades, which we called chi.com.

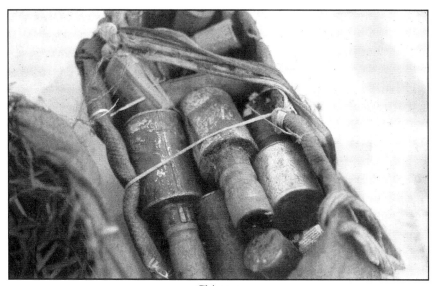

Chi.com
Courtesy of David Forsyth

The Black Market was very prevalent. Sometimes we bought military equipment from them. Once in a while we bought beer from them. It was no Budweiser, but it was beer.

When I arrived at battalion headquarters, I was lead to a hootch (portable plywood, screened barracks with a steel roof) and was told that I would be spending the night there. As I picked out a cot and stored my gear, the Staff Sergeant that I had met on the plane walked in to greet me. I was happy to see him, as it was a familiar face. It is hard to go to such a foreign place and not know anyone. It is a very desolate feeling. As we were talking, a Warrant Officer walked in and said, "I need two more people to man a tank". A Warrant Officer is an enlisted man who worked his way up from enlisted to the rank of officer. They were also called Mustangs. They had more respect than anyone else in the Marine Corps. The Staff Sergeant said he would volunteer. He looked in my direction and said I would volunteer also. I felt myself cringe.

Everyone knows that you do not volunteer for anything!

We met the two other members that were going to make up the four man crew, mounted up, and were on our way. This is the first and only time I was sent on a mission with only one tank. We usually worked in twos, threes, or fives like a gang of bullies. The Staff Sergeant had all of the information that was needed. There was a tower overlooking the hill manned by twelve grunts. We were to support it. The grunts in the tower had communications with headquarters in Da Nang. If the enemy came our way, we were to warn Da Nang.

My thoughts were interrupted by heavy artillery firing overhead which is a sound I will never forget. I thought, "I hope our artillery doesn't screw up and have a short round", which is not having enough powder, causing the round to drop shorter than anticipated.

The grunts in the tower spotted a North Vietnamese soldier on the other side of the river watching something with binoculars. They called in to ask permission for the tank to fire on him. The message came back that we could not fire on him because there was an American patrol near him.

The Staff Sergeant climbed the tower to take a look around and to talk to the grunts. He returned some time later with a very solemn look on his face. He said that the grunts received an intelligence report. There was a battalion of North Vietnamese soldiers heading our way. They had civilians in front. We had a total of sixteen Marines and a single tank to hold off a battalion of at least hundreds of North Vietnamese regular soldiers. Regular soldiers were well trained and well equipped soldiers. The Viet Cong were more like militia. In our present situation, I thought we would last a few seconds. I asked the Staff Sergeant if we would get reinforcements. He said, "I doubt it. Don't worry about it. Get some sleep and I will take the first watch". It was Tet which is a month long Chinese New Year, and the North was on the move.

It is an odd feeling thinking that you are going to die in a few hours. A warm breeze brushed over me. It felt good flowing over my sweaty body. It was a sharp contrast to what was running through my mind. I was barely old enough to drink in the US, but soon I was going to die for it. I felt a sorrow for my brother and sisters, my parents, and my friends. I thought about the girl I had back home. How would they take my death? I thought about the people back home. When they read the newspaper, would they say, "He couldn't last two days over there. What a loser."

When the North Vietnamese soldiers would come, they would not come up the hill. They would go around us in the gullies to our sides and come around from behind. It really didn't matter how they came to us. There were enough of them to annihilate us in minutes. They would take a lot of casualties. The tank can put out a lot of rounds in a short time, but it was inevitable that we would last a short time just from shear numbers.

I thought about a movie I had seen on the Alamo and their heroic stand. I thought about my heroic stand. Standing on top of the tank firing my .45 down to the second to the last bullet. The last bullet was for me. However, no one would know about this last stand. I knew it wouldn't go that way. I chose the position of loader on the tank so I could sit on top and see the scenery on the way there. As loader, I would be down inside the turret with the hatch open to throw out the empty ninety millimeter brass and let some of the gas from firing the main gun out. I would be choking, and my nose and eyes would be running.

I really was not too afraid. I knew when the time came, I would be so busy and pumped up with adrenalin, that it would happen quickly. A statement from jungle training that stuck in my mind was, "Always save one bullet. No matter what happens, don't be taken alive." The only thing that would prevent a massacre was reinforcements, and they weren't coming. It was inevitable.

As night closed in, the shelling stopped. Soon I heard a plane and saw a fluorescent red rope falling from the dark sky. What the hell is that? I was told it was Puff, but not to worry because it was one of ours. Puff was short for Puff the Magic Dragon. It was a C130 flown and operated by the Air Force. It was fitted with two miniguns which protruded from both sides of the fuselage. There were two of these C130's in Vietnam. We called one Puff and the other one Spooky. I think every fifth round is a tracer, but it looks like a solid rope because there were so many rounds.

I was surprised to see green tracers going back up towards the plane. Americans used red tracers, and the NVA (North Vietnamese Army) used green. They were either very brave, very protected, or very stupid to shoot back at that plane.

Then, a single artillery round fired. I heard a loud popping noise and the whole area lit up like daylight. It was an artillery flair. Some time later, more of the area was constantly lit by the very bright flares - then some much larger flares. It was so bright. I was amazed how lit up the area was. I was afraid we would lose our night vision. They were being dropped by planes. I could see the large parachutes as they came toward the earth, making a strange, woofing sound with smoke streaming from the flare. Then there was an artillery barrage which is when they fire all of their guns at a certain area for a long period of time. It lasted for quite a while. Then all was quiet.

I settled down on the engine plating on the back of the tank. It was not comfortable but better than the ground and much better than some places I would sleep in the near future. As I tried to fall asleep, I said my silent prayer, "Please God, I know I will never go home alive from this place, so please, when my time comes, please let me go with dignity and not screaming and crying in pain and agony." With more time spent in the country, I would add to my daily prayer, "Please do not let me do something stupid and get some of my people killed or wounded."

I finally drifted off to sleep only to be awakened for my watch. I was surprised that I could even fall asleep. Again, it seemed so quiet and peaceful. The stars were beautiful. It seemed like I saw more shooting stars than I had ever seen back home. Even with the anxiety of the danger, I felt so lonely. I was surrounded by people but longed for the voice and softness of a woman to take away the loneliness. It was something that I would desire for almost a year. What else do you think about when you are all alone at night, and it is peaceful and quiet?

During my watch, I stared as intently as possible in the darkness. I knew that in the tower they had a starlight scope. It allows you to see in the darkness. It has a green image and not much definition but you can pick up movement with it very well.

I definitely did not want the Battalion of North Vietnamese to slip up on us and for me not to see it, but it was so damned dark that it almost seemed useless. What about behind us? I haven't looked in that direction much. I wondered how close they were. How soon will the end come? How will it all play out?

After my watch, I once again drifted off to sleep wondering when the North Vietnamese would get there. In the morning, I awoke to the sun coming up. It was astonishing! Again, I was taken back by how serene and peaceful it seemed in the midst of it all. Morning is a nice time in Vietnam. It is not too hot. The animals are waking in the jungle and starting to call. I could hear the monkeys mostly. I could hear the insects making their buzzing noises and the birds chirping. The sun takes away the night coolness. "What happened to the North Vietnamese?" I asked the Staff Sergeant. He had no idea either.

On the outside, I didn't say anything. On the inside I was ecstatic to be alive. How could this have happened? Where did they go? Thank you, God! What a strange feeling. Last night I thought it was a sure death, but today a bright sun and warm C rations greeted me. Life was good!

We never found out what happened to the North Vietnamese soldiers, but I didn't really care. I was alive and it was my third day in Vietnam.

303,704 were reported wounded in Vietnam
153,329 were hospitalized
150,375 were injured requiring no hospital care
75,000 were severely disabled
23,204 were 100% disabled
5,283 were lost or severely impaired limbs
1,081 were sustained multiple amputations

Amputation or crippling wounds to the lower extremities were 300% higher than in WWII and 70% higher than Korea. (Expanded use of land mines)

Tanks

Tanks in Vietnam! The Marine Corps has a Fleet Marine Force, or FMF, with a Battalion Landing Team. Each Battalion Landing Team has a full regiment of grunts and all support groups, which include tanks. When one of these BLTs was sent to Vietnam, they naturally took the tanks with them.

This started a huge controversy. It was felt by many that tanks were not suitable for the territory in Vietnam. They felt that the sand, mud, and jungle were not a good fit for tanks. They were afraid that the tanks would get bogged down in the sand and mud, and in the jungle you could not defend yourself because everything was so closed in. Also by having tanks in Vietnam, it was thought to have escalated the war. Prior to the tanks, there were just advisors there. Now we were making a statement by bringing in the tanks.

The tank we used in the USMC was called an M48-A3, and it was considered a medium tank. It is called a Patton by our Army cousins. I once saw a platoon of heavy tanks at the tank park in Camp Lejeune, North Carolina. I never saw them move. They would sometimes break a torsion bar just sitting there, so the suspension system was inadequate for the weight it carried. To my knowledge, they were the only heavy tanks in existence at that time. They weighed sixty four tons. They had a 120 millimeter main gun and two loaders - one for the powder and one for the projectile. The M-67 flame tank was a medium tank, but the turret was modified to carry napalm. It carried about three hundred gallons of napalm. We escorted these guys on many operations.

The M48-A3, the tank we used, was equipped with sixty two rounds of ninety millimeter ammo for the main gun, which came in a variety of types - high explosive, high explosive anti-tank, white phosphorus, flechette, and canister. A canister round had 2200 pellets, approximately half of an inch in diameter. A flechette round contained 4400 darts, approximately 1/8 inch round and one inch long and made of stainless steel. It also had an adjustable fuse that caused the round to burst either coming out of the main gun or up to 4400 meters away or anywhere in between, depending on the desired setting. White phosphorus or willie peter was a chemical round that would burn anything it touched after fired. A high explosive antitank round was called a HEAT round. It was made for tanks, but we used it for bunkers and other things. A high explosive was our old standby. It had a few tenths of a second delay, so it would explode inside the bunker instead of outside the bunker on impact. In heavy combat, we were not too concerned with what we sent them, as long as it came quickly. All the ninety millimeter rounds were stored in the turret or within easy reach of the turret.

The tank had a range finder, which was in the tank commander's position. It was very fast and easy to use. When we looked through the tank commander's sight we would see two images. We would turn a small crank and it would bring the two images together. When they were together and very clear, we had our range.

The next step to fire the ninety millimeter was to key in the type of round to be fired into the ballistic computer. The computer would raise the gun tube or ninety millimeter gun to compensate for the amount of drop in the round and range.

Tank Firing
Courtesy of David Forsyth

The tank, fully loaded, weighed about 53.2 tons. It was powered by a 750 horse diesel (V 12 or 12 cylinders) engine. It was governed to limit speeds to thirty miles per hour. When turning at a higher speed it had a tendency to roll over. Its shape was angles and curves. A large round had to hit almost perfectly to penetrate, otherwise it would ricochet off of the side. In many cases the ricochet would be harmful to the crew men, because it would carry shrapnel from the tank itself, added to the force of the original ammo and possibly strike the crew men. The hull was made of homogeneous steel, which made it much harder. Thickness varied depending on the location on the tank, heaviest in the front, lighter in the back. The hull was two to four inches thick. The turret was seven inches thick in the front, three inches thick on the sides, and two inches in the back.

The driver was located in the front of the hull. He was by himself up there. There was an escape hatch under him. He had a hatch where he could put his head out to see as much as possible. He could close the hatch and use the periscopes to drive, too. If the turret was traversed to the rear he could climb through a small opening into the turret. The tank had a shift lever for high range (high speed), low range (slower speed), neutral, and reverse. It had a, sort of, butterfly shaped steering wheel. You could do what was called a neutral steer by putting the tank shift lever into neutral and turning the steering wheel in either direction and step on the throttle. One track would go forward and one track would go backwards. It would turn on a dime, so to speak. The driver was usually the second man in experience.

The tank commander (the senior man on the tank who was also called a TC) had a hatch in the copula on top of the turret. It looked like a clam shell, and so it was called a clam shell hatch. The copula had lots of periscopes but gave limited vision if the tank was totally buttoned up (buttoned up is where all the hatches are closed and locked down). The tank commander had an override to take over from the gunner and could take control of the main gun if desired. He had a much better view and could make better decisions on targets than the gunner could.

There was a seat that the tank commander could stand on,

where he would be half exposed and have a great view of what was going on. For long, non-dangerous rides, he could sit on the clam shell. Most of the tanks were equipped with what was called a sky mounted fifty caliber machine gun. This was in complete control of the tank commander. I also carried an M16 on the back of my tank. I was always a good shot with a rifle, and sometimes the machine guns would jam. Then I would grab the M16. I would also grab it if I saw a small portion of a target. Someone peeking through the brush only exposing themselves in very small portions. Some people complained about the M16. I know I had a newer version of it, and it never failed me. I picked it up from someone who didn't need it anymore. I carried it on the back of the tank in the racks. It was exposed to rain and dust, and it never failed to fire. I wish I could have taken it home with me. I remember thinking so many times, while firing the fifty caliber machine gun, that if you only had a rifle that had this caliber, it would be awesome, but the recoil would probably almost kill you.

The loader stood on the left side of the main gun. He was usually the newest person on the crew. His job was to load rounds into the main gun and tend the thirty caliber machine gun co-mounted with the main gun. The gunner had his choice of main gun or thirty caliber machine gun.

Behind the main gun there were the radios and a protective

Marine Corps Tank in Vietnam

guard to prevent the rounds of the main gun from hitting the radios as they ejected. The main gun was on a hydraulic system and came back into the turret when fired. If, by chance, someone would get behind the main gun when firing, he would be crushed.

The gunner sat beside the main gun in the turret on the right side. His job was to control the main gun and the coaxially mounted thirty caliber machine gun.

Tanks were very large. They were almost eleven feet tall, twelve feet wide, and twenty nine feet long. The tracks were twenty eight inches wide. I spent quite a bit of time with them for the next year.

I remember hearing that one of the tanks in our platoon had gotten stuck so badly that they had two tanks in front of it trying to pull it out and a large helicopter pulling up to try to free it and it would not come out. They finally ordered lumber in and pulled it out with two tanks. I was not involved with this mess. I just listened over the radios.

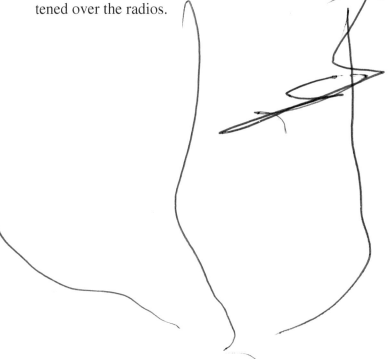

The Village of Nui Kim Sahn

We had two primary bases of operation, Battalion Headquarters, which was on a hill outside of Da Nang, on the southwest
side of the city, and Charlie Company Headquarters, which was
south of Marble Mountain. Battalion Headquarters was where the
supplies came from and where the tactical operations were con-
ducted. It had three tank companies; of which we were one, and a
headquarters company, which was maintenance. Charlie Company
Headquarters was where we had three tank platoons, of which we
were one. We rotated from one of them to the other as well as in
the field on different operations and locations.

I spent a day and a half at Battalion Headquarters. We headed to Charlie Company Headquarters by Jeep. As we were driving
along the roads, I still had no idea what I was heading into. I asked
the driver some questions, but there was so much going through
my mind, I couldn't ask him all of them. It was about a twenty
mile drive.

Charlie Company Headquarters
Courtesy of David Forsyth

When I finally got to Company Headquarters and was shown around, it was late in the day. A Staff Sergeant told me that I would have to put up a rack in the squad bay until they had room in the Sergeant's quarters. It was dark by now. There was no one around so I decided to hit the rack early. Who knows what tomorrow would bring. I fell asleep and was soon awakened by a group of guys coming back from the enlisted men's club. I did not feel too social as they were drinking heavily, and I was not. I pretended to be sleeping. The conversation turned to me. Someone said, "Does anyone know what he's like?" and I heard the reply, "I hear he is a wuss". It kind of pissed me off. I later learned that when you first got to Vietnam, nobody had respect for you. After a long time, you earned their respect, and then their loyalty is forever.

The next day I was assigned a tank and crew. Then I was told that I was going to accompany a tank commanded by a Corporal to a nearby friendly village. They wanted to keep it friendly, so a tank was parked on the road at each end of the village to protect them.

As darkness came, the Corporal asked me to come with him. He led me to a hootch, which is a hut that is actually rice straw woven into a roof and walls. It had a dirt floor and a small bamboo bed in the corner. It looked a lot like the Brooklyn Gang hut back home. There were no tables or chairs. In fact, the only chairs I ever remember seeing in Vietnam were in the city of Da Nang. There were small rice bowls and sometimes a teapot or a small coffee pot for heating water hanging on the bamboo frames of the walls. There was a small wood fire burning in the middle of the room. To this day I will smell that same type of wood-burning smell, and I will quickly remember the hootches with their fire inside. All hootches were made like this one. A fire in a grass hooch seemed a little unsafe to me, but it worked for them. There were always four or five people squatting around the fire. That is how they all sat, no chairs - just squatting instead of sitting. All of the adults in the village wore what we called black pajamas and a woven rice straw hat when outside. The young girls wore white outfits called Ao Dai's. I never understood how they kept them so clean. They all wore sandals. Sometimes they would go barefoot, but mostly they were in sandals and never shoes.

The Corporal brought some gifts (soap and smokes) for the girl he was seeing. I sat with them for a while, but I felt very uncomfortable with the situation, especially since we were all three sitting on the bed (remember, no chairs). I did not know what these guys were used to, but I was in charge of a tank and crew on the other side of the village. I felt very strongly that I needed to be with them. In broken English, the girl said to me, "Why are you so quiet? You look like you are home sick." I soon left and went back to my responsibilities. I don't ever remember entering another Vietnamese hootch.

The children were something else. When I got back to my tank there were several children gathered around it. Most spoke English very well. I asked the guys about the children. They said that they always hung out with the tankers. I was sent there every night for a couple of weeks. I got used to the children, and they got used to me. One seemed to adopt me. He must have been about six or seven years old. Everywhere I went, he was there. It got to the point when I ate, he ate. I would share my C rations with him and the others. It was nice to have the happy little guys around.

Once as we passed through one village, a little girl was standing there. She was probably four or five years old. She looked so cute. I tossed her a can of C rations. She just stood there looking at the big Americans and the big tanks passing by. She didn't pick up the food. As we passed through the village on other occasions, she was right there at the same spot. I tossed her another can. Same results. Soon the other tankers with me joined in and all the village kids ran to gather up the C rations, except her. She just didn't get it. Her mother did, though, and was quick to retrieve the can. I think there was only one time I passed the village when the little girl was not there. I thought to myself that I wish I could take some of the children home and give them a better life.

As soon as the sun rose, we were awakened by the chatter of the people, and the smell of the cooking fires filled our senses. The children arrived soon after the sun was up. Well, at least the ones who didn't sleep on the tanks with us did. The people of the village had very little, but seemed to enjoy life. They seemed to have all they wanted or needed - a simple but happy life. I actually admired them for their simple, effective way of living. We Americans have so much but never seem to be happy. We just want more, but they seemed content with the little they had.

The Children of Nui Kim Sahn
Courtesy of Gary Mefford

Many of the people I served with hated the Vietnamese. They felt that they were all enemies and should be exterminated. They talked about the boat method. You take all the good Vietnamese and put them on boats, kill all the rest, and then sink the boats. I felt that the Vietnamese were fighting for their own land and country. I am sure some friendly villages were set up by the enemy who would intentionally place a mine near the village. At times the North would send executioners into a friendly village, take young males for their military, and would threaten to come back to kill their families if they didn't cooperate. They would take what they wanted from the villagers. They would make the villagers do things against Americans. The North would have the villagers plant mines and booby traps. Then, when the villagers harassed us, we would retaliate against them. The villagers were just like pawns to the North. It did not seem like a fair game to me.

Nui Kim Sahn was small compared to some - probably two hundred people. There was an ARVN (Army of the Republic of Vietnam) platoon stationed there. We did little socializing with them. They would stare at us as they went by, but they didn't seem to like us much. They were in and out of the village constantly. You could not help wondering which side they were on.

I heard from someone that Battalion got hit one night. They were raided by at least forty or fifty North Vietnamese sympathizers. In the morning they found the Battalion barber in the concertina wire (Concertina wire was like barbed wire, only it had more edges and was triple strands of wire). It was placed around a compound to slow the enemy's advance. He was shot trying to kill us Americans. What a great spot to plant a spy, in the local barber shop to hear and see everything. I remember getting a shave from him when I was back at Battalion. When he was done cutting your hair he would wrap a warm towel around your face then lather it up and sharpen the straight razor on a leather strap. It felt good, but I didn't like him that close to my throat with a sharp razor. I guess my instincts were right on.

Moving bodies after an attack
Courtesy of Gary Mefford

I stayed in the mud flats (which is what we called the area because it was a huge, swampy, muddy flatland) for about three months. While I was enjoying my stay in the mud flats, the road was changed and no longer passed by the village. When I returned to Company Headquarters, everything looked so very different. We now had a dirt road that seemed like a real road. It was now called the MSR or military supply route. The road and the term were very new to me. I remember the road being very narrow, with vegetation growing very close to it. I never got to return to that village again. I wonder what ever happened to my little buddy and the little girl who just stood there.

When the North Vietnamese took power in the south they were not too fond of people who associated with Americans. Some were executed, some sent to reform farms, where they were "reindoctrinated" (brainwashed), and some were sent to prisons where they were kept until someone paid a ransom for them.

I also talked to a tanker that I served with who adopted a little girl while he was in Vietnam. That is what we called it when a kid hung out with us all of the time. He returned to Vietnam many years later to find out that she died during childbirth. He also said that the people were very friendly toward him, even the people who had been our enemies in the past.

During my first week, I was with a two tank operation going to the village. There was a Staff Sergeant on my tank. He was on the loader's hatch and I was on the TC's. We were very close to Company Headquarters. For some reason that I don't recall we stopped, and the Staff Sergeant dismounted. Soon after, we started getting incoming mortar fire. The first one was very close, and I saw the Staff Sergeant fall to the ground. The second was off into the jungle, and the third was close again. They were working on their range. He yelled up to me to return fire, which I did with the fifty caliber sky mounted machine gun. A few bursts of rounds and it was all over. Luckily the Staff Sergeant was not injured. Those incidents happened so fast and frequently. It is amazing how you can be so relaxed one minute and so pumped up on adrenaline in the next one.

I was the second of two tanks traveling near the village.

The other tank was commanded by a Sergeant, but he was in the country longer and knew what was going on better than I did. Right next to the village in a small water puddle, he hit a mine. It was not a large one and no one was hurt; but one of the tank tracks was damaged. In twenty minutes, we had the track repaired, and we were on our way again. This was our friendly local village. Was the mine put there to make it look like it was planted by a villager?

I was sitting on a berm (four foot high embankment around the perimeter of the village) talking to a grunt. It was a dark, starry night. I told him that it gets pretty boring here sometimes. He said "Watch this!" and opened fire with his M16. Soon the whole encampment was shooting at nothing. It was a pretty sight to see all the tracers and knowing there was not an attack coming. I wondered what the enemy thought at those times - "crazy Americans shooting at nothing." I also wondered, what was the cost in dollars for this incident.

Soon after I came to our Company Headquarters, I was told I could use the Staff and Officer's Club. I went on several occasions but felt much more comfortable at the Enlisted Men's Club.

One of the guys told me he and some of the other guys got together to write a letter. He said it pertained to me. When I asked him about it, he refused to say what it was. About two weeks later, I received a type written letter and an autographed photo of Racquel Welch. I still have them. I never knew what the guys wrote to her, but I thought it was really cool that I got a letter and a picture back.

On another occasion we were escorting a grunt patrol, who were doing a sweep operation near the road to our Company Headquarters. This was the road between our village and Company Headquarters. There was a grunt on foot in front of my tank. He was probably twenty feet in front of me. I was watching him as he stepped on an antipersonnel mine. The expression on his face never changed.

He walked in a circle and fell over right in front of my tank. When he fell, I could barely see him because he was so close to the front of the tank. A Corpsman quickly came to his aid and a jeep with a driver and another Corpsman pulled up to us on the road. As the two Corpsman put their arms around his shoulder and helped him to the road, all three stepped on another small antipersonnel mine. The rest of the grunts helped them in the jeep and they drove away. I never saw them again, but I don't think that grunt even knew what happened to him. Thinking back, he probably lived, but I am sure he lost his foot.

We were rotated to different positions throughout I-corps area. Once, while it was our platoon's time to be at Battalion Head-quarters, the Communications Sergeant (or Company Communications Chief) asked if I wanted to go for a ride. He had access to a jeep and needed to check on the communications system at Company Headquarters. He told me that this is where we would move to soon. He was a real character. He could talk his way into and out of anything. For some reason he had some Lieutenant bars. No one wore rank insignias in Vietnam. The higher rank you were the bigger the target. I knew this guy would be successful in life because he had a great ability to speak with anyone at any level. He was a great talker.

The road to Company Headquarters was mined so heavily that it was swept by a team of engineers every morning. There were guards at the beginning and the end of the road to stop everyone from passing on an unswept road. On this occasion we came to a guard who did nothing so we felt it was safe to continue. About halfway down the road we met the team coming up the road. They stopped us and said, "What the hell are you guys doing? The road is not swept!" I said nothing but prayed a silent prayer. The Communications Sergeant turned the jeep around, drove a short way (in the same tracks) away from the team, stopped, and put on the Lieutenant bars. He went back and chewed the hell out of that dumb ass guard. The guards said nothing but, "Yes sir". I actually felt bad for him when the Sergeant (with the Lieutenant bars) was done with him, although, I never understood why he didn't do anything to warn us.

The Mud Flats

We had an Am Trk (Amphibious Tractor Battalion) platoon in our Company Headquarters. An Am Trk is a large square personnel carrier. It had a large heavy gate up front that had been known to crush people if they were not quick enough to get out of the way.

They actually floated, and I was told, according to engineers, that it would not float. I saw them travel rivers and come off of ships loaded with troops. Only about a foot of the top of it was visible while in water. I saw them come off of ships, and they would disappear under water for a while. I heard the grunts that they were carrying would go berserk for a while because they thought they were sinking. They had thin armor compared to a tank and were gasoline powered which meant they would burn very easily when they hit a mine or received small arms fire in the right place.

AmTrk's at Charlie Company Headquarters
Courtesy of David Forsyth

There was a Staff Sergeant in charge of the platoon. He was a good Sergeant. I escorted him on several operations. He and I got along well, and I never knew if he requested me or it was coincidence that I went on so many operations with him.

During a briefing just prior to an operation, he and I were discussing tactics with a grunt colonel who wanted my friend to take his Am Trks down a river to a very dangerous area. The Colonel said, "I want you to take the Am Trks down the river along this area", pointing to a map.

"That is almost suicide!" the Staff Sergeant retorted.

The Colonel replied carelessly, "They are obsolete anyway and will be phased out soon". He did not seem to care about the lives in them.

On another operation I was escorting the Am Trk's along a dirt road. I was off the road about one hundred feet and the Am Trks were about fifty feet from me, when the Staff Sergeant's Am Trk hit a mine. It started to burn. There was not much we could do except watch it burn. Luckily everyone got out alive, although the Staff Sergeant had a minor wound. He said to me, "Blow that hooch away." There was a grass shack about fifty feet off the opposite side of the road and directly in line with the mine. I had the gunner fire a ninety millimeter round HE (high explosive) into the hooch. I think to this day the people in the hooch were probably innocent and the mine was planted by the Viet Cong.

Am Trk after hitting a mine

Eventually the Staff Sergeant received his third Purple Heart and was sent home, but not before he had his fun with me.

He was always getting wounded but fortunately never seriously.

I was told I was going to the Mud Flats. I had no idea what it was or where it was. When I asked about it I was told it was a real bad area. It was known as little Khe Sanh. It was totally enemy controlled. It was also a free fire zone which meant we could fire on anything we felt the need to without asking permission. It was also a Korean Marine area. The Koreans did not have tanks in Vietnam, so we were attached to them. I had heard rumors of the Korean Marines being a very tough outfit. I heard they all had to be at least a brown belt in martial arts.

The Staff Sergeant looked at me and said, "You're going to the Mud Flats. That's a really bad area. You will never survive out there. You are a dead man." After days of teasing me about this, he came back from an operation and told me he had something to show me. We walked out to the tank park where a crowd of people were all laughing. There was a tombstone on the back of my tank. It was a real tombstone. It was white with big black letters. It said, "Rest in Peace Sgt. Hoch". Everyone got a good laugh out of it. I know there are some photos of it in existence somewhere. I do not know what ever happened to it, but it disappeared after a couple of weeks. I have to admit that the Staff Sergeant was making me think.

I was then told that I was going to leadership school back in Da Nang. TAD again. I didn't want to go. I wanted to stay with my outfit. I was told that there was time, and I had no choice but to go. I could complete the school and be back in time to go to the Mud Flats.

The school turned out to be a great experience. It is one of the finest schools I have ever attended. The head instructor was an old Gunnery Sergeant who taught at the Marine Corps Officer Candidate School. The days were very long - up at four thirty in the morning, and sometimes the classes lasted until nine or ten at night for two weeks. I was glad I went and remember to this day the Gunny said, "If you are going to give someone shit put yourself in his place and think about that before you spout off". I was glad I went to this school.

After looking at a map of the Mud Flats I saw our compound would be right on highway four. How bad could the area be if it was on a highway? I soon learned that highway four was only on the map. The road itself had not been used for years. All the bridges we saw were blown up. The highway was not even a foot path. It was all overgrown. In fact, a month or so later, I built a bunker in the middle of highway four. As we traveled through the bush, I kept looking for the highway.

Finally, we were on our way to the Mud Flats. After several miles of dirt road we met up with a Korean Marine patrol. We headed into the bush. After about an hour we came to a small stream. It looked like a good place to cross, as it was well used by others who had crossed. We had a USMC engineer attached to us just for this operation and for this purpose. It was a perfect place for a mine. It was about mid day and hot, and we were tired and hungry.

The night before, some of the guys were at the enlisted men's club at C Company Headquarters. The club consisted of a plywood hooch. It had a plywood floor, a plywood and tin roof, and plywood sides about four feet up. The rest was screening on the sides. They were the same as we lived in back at headquarters. They were up off the ground a couple of feet, which was necessary in the monsoon season. The engineer was at the club and told the guys that when this operation was over, he wanted to turn in his mine detector because it would cut out for just a second every once in a while.

I thought this was a good time to open a can of C rations. C rations in Vietnam were mostly left over from World War II and were not bad for the first week of eating them. They consisted of a variety of different meals plus peanut butter and crackers or cheese and crackers, always a five pack of smokes, Chicklets, and toilet paper.

I sat on the top of the turret eating my cold C rations and watching the engineer sweep for mines. There were two Korean Marines next to him, one on each side. I saw the explosion. I did not see the engineer as the blast engulfed him. I saw the two Koreans both fly in the air and do a cart wheel in harmony. Both Koreans were dead and one was put on the back of each of the two tanks. There were pieces of bloody clothing that was smoking all over my tank from the engineer. All that was found of him was placed in a poncho, rolled up, and put on the back of my tank. I was told it was an antitank mine, and it left a very large crater. All were dead, and there were no wounded so there was not a big hurry to get a MedEvac in.

We crossed at a different spot and were on our way. Soon we arrived at a small compound of sand bag bunkers and a sand bag perimeter. Nothing was above ground. Home sweet home! There were openings at each end of the compound where we parked the tanks. There was no vegetation for about two hundred yards around the compound. Each tank crew had a small bunker of its own. The first few days were uneventful, and we were just getting used to our new friends. What a cultural difference!

We were about 14,000 meters from our nearest friendlies. We didn't know exactly where they were located or who they were. Here we lived underground. We withstood countless attacks from mortars, rockets, and small arms. I do not recall anyone being seriously wounded from these attacks. Most of our wounded came from operations outside the compound.

On many occasions the North Vietnamese talked to the Koreans with loud speakers. Always during these sessions the Koreans had a strained look on their faces, a look of fear. I would sometimes ask the Koreans what the North Vietnamese said. They would tell me they said, "We are the same type of people, don't support the evil Americans!" I would worry that we may have an uprising from the Koreans. The North Vietnamese would do this sometimes for hours. I was glad when they stopped.

The Mud flats were the base for many search and destroy missions. Some of the ones we were involved in were major operations, but we didn't know the names of or the results of the operations. The Korean Captain was fairly tight lipped with information to us so I had no idea what the big picture was. A big thing for the big guys in the rear was enemy body counts. We sometimes took credit for a kill or two, but most of the time we didn't care about kill numbers. I have a certificate that credits me with six enemy confirmed kills. There were many more.

The area where we spent most of our time was called the rocket belt, where rockets were launched for Da Nang. Rockets usually came in two varieties, one hundred twenty millimeters and one hundred forty millimeters. They were set up on bamboo platforms and usually launched in sets of four - usually twelve in a session. Then another group would start.

On one evening we saw a set of four rockets launched about two hundred yards away. We fired the ninety millimeter main gun at them with a standard high explosive round. We saw two more rockets launch. Again we fired. We saw one more rocket launch, and all was quiet. I cannot say for sure that we prevented some of the rockets from reaching Da Nang, but from our perspective, it sure looked like it. I do not think we passed this information on to our Platoon Commander.

I was also on the receiving end of the rockets at Battalion Headquarters. Once, while on guard duty late at night, I heard them coming. It was too late to do anything. I heard them pass over my head and hit behind me in Da Nang. Soon I heard the sirens go off in Da Nang. I wished I could have gone down to see the destruction the next day.

This area was also known as a transit area for troops traveling to the Da Nang area off the Ho Che Min Trail. The troops we usually encountered were well trained, well equipped, and determined. We seldom encountered the famed Viet Cong.

MedEvac Chopper Near Charlie Company Headquarters
Courtesy of Gary Mefford

Battalion Headquarters
Courtesy of Gary Mefford

Air Strike at Marble Mountain
Courtesy of David Forsyth

MedEvac Choppers
Courtesy of Gary Mefford

Tanks at Charlie Company Headquarters
Courtesy of Gary Mefford

Grunts on a Tank as it Fires

Getting Ready to Go
Courtesy of David Forsyth

The Village of Nui Kim Sahn
Courtesy of Gary Mefford

Mud Flats: Search and Destroy Mission

We started out on another search and destroy mission with the ROK (Republic of Korea) Marines. We traveled for some time before we ran into a village. There were no friendlies in this area, so it was an abandoned outlaw village or base camp for the NVA (North Vietnamese Army). It must have recently been abandoned because there were fires still going with rice cooking over them. The ROK Marines burned the hootches, shot up the area, and killed the chickens and pigs. We were in the tanks, so we just sat and watched. They asked us if they could put a large dead pig on my tank. I said sure, thinking some fresh meat would go down good tonight. It would be a nice change from WWII C rations.

The ROK Marines ate kim che and rice almost every meal. Kim che is cabbage that is buried in the ground with spices and left to ferment for months. It was terrible having to use their latrines. The smell was unbearable. The ROK Marines cooked rice in ammo boxes. This worked quite well, except once. The ROK Marine doing the cooking didn't take out the rubber seal, which kept moisture from getting into the rounds. The rubber formed an airtight seal, and the can exploded. He had to be MedEvaced out. I have had kim che and rice many times. It is very spicy and hot. It is not a good breakfast meal.

After quite some time, and the burning of probably sixteen hootches, we started to move on. Towards afternoon we approached a large field with low grass. The ROK Marines seemed to be moving very slowly and very cautiously. They were slightly in front of us and spread out to the sides of the tanks. We were spaced so that both of the tanks could easily cover the other tank. There was a jungle directly in front of us. About halfway through the field, I heard an explosion. I looked in that direction and saw dirt and debris on the other side of the other tank. It was low on the other tank, and I wrongly assumed they had hit a mine.

I sat and waited to see if it would develop into an attack. It was my job to cover the other tank if this would be the case. I sat and waited some more. Soon I saw an ROK medic carry someone away from the tank. It looked like the driver. They were too far away to tell for sure. Then the radio cracked with a broken message from the other tank. I couldn't understand what the other Tank Commander was saying.

Luckily, on this particular operation, we had a Staff Sergeant with us, so he was in charge. This took loads of pressure off of me. He was in the tank to my right, so whatever happened now, it was all his call. He was calling over the radios and I had no idea what he was saying. We started to take a lot of small arms fire. I replied to his broken up messages. "Wait one." I took off my tank helmet and ran across the opened field, climbed up on the side of his tank so he could tell me what was going on. I found out that they had been hit by two rocket propelled grenades. One penetrated low in the hull. The other hit the turret and ricocheted as they were traversing. The shrapnel hit the driver in the back of the head, shoulders, back, arms, and the top of the thighs. He was about my age. The driver had one of those Southern personalities. He was really easy going and soft spoken, always polite. He was one of those people that everyone takes to right away. He was MedEvaced out, and I did not see him again until many years later. At the time, I didn't know if he lived or died. For many years I wondered about it.

I thought the RPG (rocket propelled grenade) disrupted the radios and the electronic control to traverse the turret. The turret could be moved manually, but it was difficult and slow.

I ran back to my tank, not wanting it to be without a Commander for too long. I told my driver to go to the other tank and drive for them. I felt that since the other tank was partially disabled, they should have a full crew. I told my loader he was now the driver. I asked an ROK Lieutenant if he could give me someone who could speak English to load the main gun for us. Soon a Korean Corpsman jumped up on the tank. I told him to go down the loader's hatch. I met him inside. I started to explain to him what to do. He looked around and jumped out. Next came an ROK Lieutenant. He jumped in, looked around, and jumped out also. Next came a Private. He looked scared to death and didn't seem like he was even listening to me; but apparently he had to stay because he had the lowest rank.

This photo is of the actual hole the RPG made in the side of the tank
Photo courtesy of Ralph Schwartz

We were ready to fire the main gun with a point and motion loader. It was time to fire the main gun. Unfortunately, I don't think the Private was ready. In the meantime, the gunner was working the thirty caliber machine gun. In front of us were some small humps in the ground. I figured that they were probably graves. The Vietnamese buried their people sitting down and just covered them with dirt, making a hump in the ground. You could tell the newer ones by the horrendous odor.

There were two ROK Marines lying behind some humps. They were probably thirty feet in front of the tank. I yelled to them to get away. They looked at me like I was crazy. They had found a good safe place to get comfortable. I yelled again. I know what muzzle blast can do at close range. It can burn your skin, break your eardrums, or give you a concussion. Obviously these soldiers had no idea what it could do. I yelled again and this time motioned to them with my hands to get away. They just looked at me. I did not know if they did not move because they were so scared, they did not know what to do, or if they felt safe where they were. I had no choice and fired a high explosive round from the main gun. After watching the round explode on target, I looked down and saw no signs of the ROK Marines. They must have hauled ass as soon as the ninety millimeter fired.

I told the gunner to point to a canister round to get the Korean to load into the main gun. He had to leave his gunner's position to help the ROK Marine load the round. I took over his duties from my position. We fired the canister round which is like a big shot gun shell used for antipersonnel. Next I told the gunner to have the ROK Marine load a flechette round and set the delay for one hundred feet. The round burst opened at the desired setting spreading 4400 little darts. When this round fired you could see hundreds of leaves falling. I could only imagine what would happen to the troops on the receiving side of this round. These darts could leave a bunch of holes in someone.

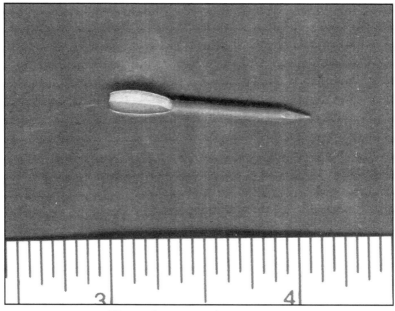

Photo of an actual flechette dart
Photo Courtesy of Ralph Schwartz

The ROK Marines had a two man detachment of US Marines called ANGLICO (Air Naval Gunfire Liaison Company). They were with the ROK Marines to call in artillery or air support when the ROK Marines needed it. They called in air support for us. In a flash, two F4 Phantom jets skimmed over the tree line, dropping what looked like six canisters each, of napalm. For those of you who do not know, napalm is a chemical mixture of gasoline and a gelling compound. When it gets on you, it sticks to you and burns your skin. The jungle lit up, huge fire balls erupted for several hundred feet, and then were gone. Twenty minutes later they were back. This time with two hundred fifty pound bombs. Each plane dropped what looked like six, and then they were gone again.

I was told, and witnessed it for myself, that you can always tell the Navy/Marine pilots from the Air Force. The Navy/Marine pilots came in at treetop level, the Air Force were very high up. It was just how they were trained. I bet the Airforce pilot's survival rate was a bit higher.

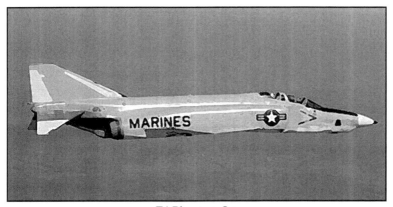

F4 Phantom Jet

To my left and in front of me, there was a small tree line. On the other side of that tree line, there was another large field. I could see troops moving toward the jungle in the direction that we were shooting. I could not tell who they were or what side they were on. I broke out the binoculars but still could not tell. I was debating whether to fire on them or not. Luckily I held off because they were friendly. I was later told by a superior that whenever you are in doubt, you need to fire. "You should not have hesitated", he told me. I disagree.

Soon the Staff Sergeant called from the other tank. His radios seemed to have improved quite a bit. He said the ROK Marines tried to flank the enemy and got caught in the field. He said he wanted me to go in and get the wounded. He would cover.

We drove out in the field under intense fire. I told the driver to drive in front of the wounded and stop so we could cover the ROK Marines as they removed the wounded. A small group of the Korean Marines followed behind the tank, using the tanks as cover.

There were six wounded lying in the field. I could see the looks on their faces as we approached. I don't think anyone was ever so happy to see us. They were not smiling, but had a look of deep gratitude on their faces. They were all wounded but still alive.

There were rocket propelled grenades and heavy small arms flying everywhere. It was like we were a magnet, attracting flying bits of metal. We did not have time to think. We were just reacting.

As the ROK Marines were loading the wounded on the back of the tank, I saw a bright flash at the edge of the jungle. I then saw a small cloud of gray smoke. The cloud of smoke started to get bigger and bigger. I soon realized that there was a small black speck in the middle of the smoke. The speck kept getting larger and larger. Then I realized that it was a rocket propelled grenade coming right for my head! This was the second weirdest experience in my life.

It was coming in slow motion. I could see it coming at me for what seemed like five minutes, and I was sure it was going to hit me right in the head. It seemed like it was taking forever, but I couldn't get out of the way. It was like being in a different time zone or dimension or something. I honestly watched as it passed just inches over my head, this black missile. I could see it so completely - it was mystifying to me. I was very puzzled by the whole situation, but I didn't have time to dwell on it. I took control of the main gun and fired in the direction of the flash.

The gunner asked what we should fire next. I said to give them a willy peter, which is a term for white phosphorous. White phosphorous is an evil round. If it gets on you, you cannot get it off. It will burn under water, mud, etc. The only thing you can do is cut it off with a knife. I felt this would give them something to think about, plus give us smoke to cover us, so we could back out.

We had loaded all of the wounded by this time.

I remember thinking that I hope to hell we did not get in any real heavy combat with the wounded on the back of the tank. They were all laid on the back of the engine plate, so if we traversed the turret, some of them would be crushed. I told the gunner that if we get into real shit, one of us was going to have to throw the wounded off rather than crush them with the turret.

Fortunately, we backed out without too much going wrong. We were just under constant fire. When we got back to the other tank and the rest of the ROK Marines, they quickly removed the wounded from the tank and moved them to stretchers. The soldiers then carried the stretchers.

The Staff Sergeant said that we were going to pull out. I said that we should pull back by leaps and bounds. It is a tanker's thing where one tank pulled back about seventy five feet behind the other tank and covered him while he moved back seventy five feet behind the other tank.

I waited until I thought the ROK Marines and the other tank had time to pull back and organize, so they could cover us as we pulled back. All the while my tank was laying down a cover fire. I told the driver of our tank to turn the tank around. As he was doing that, I planned on traversing the turret so we could still fire the main gun. This is not a good idea, as the back of the tank is the weakest point. It left the engine compartment exposed to the enemy. I felt that this was the best option of covering ourselves, the other tank, and the Koreans.

I told the driver to pass the other tank about seventy five feet and stop so we could cover them. As he was turning, I was traversing. I was still facing the direction of the enemy and the tree line. I was shocked when he said, "What other tank? I don't see one." I turned around to look and sure enough the ROK Marines and the other tank were gone. I could not believe it! We were abandoned.

As I looked back to the front of the turret, I saw a sight that not many men will ever see in their lifetime. I was the only one privileged enough to see this spectacle, as the driver was now in the front facing the opposite way. The ROK loader was down inside. If the gunner ever saw it through his sights, he never mentioned it.

It was probably what Custer felt like. I was scared to death. I saw hundreds and hundreds of the North Vietnamese Army stand up and start walking toward us. I could see that they were well equipped and all dressed alike. They were shoulder to shoulder - hundreds and hundreds of them coming toward us shouting and shooting. I said "HOLY SHIT!!".

Everyone on the crew said "What?" through the intercom.

I said to the driver, "I want you to kick it in the ass and keep it there until we are back." I will never forget the sight of all those soldiers or how I felt watching them.

As we retreated, we were firing as much as possible. We were very ineffective because the tank was going full speed and the turret was bouncing around, so the rounds were going all over the place. I was a Marine and we were taught never to retreat. Well I was retreating. I could not and did not think of anything else we could do. What could I do? I was filled with fear, anger, relief, and almost every emotion possible in a very short period of time. I would never forget the details of that day.

On the way back I thought about shooting the damned Staff Sergeant who abandoned us. I found out much later I was not the only one who thought about shooting him. Even his own men wanted to shoot him at the time. Some leaders were shot by their own men in Vietnam. What would that accomplish? I never said anything to him, but I hated him for leaving us there. I tried not taking it personally, but he was a Marine, and you do not do that to other Marines. I was told later that he put himself in for a silver star for that day. I wouldn't be surprised if he got it. The gunner of the other tank said that the Staff Sergeant just sat there the whole time and did nothing. I was told that he had a big lump on his head where a small arms round hit him in the head, but his tank helmet stopped it. I also found out that there was nothing wrong with the radios when we were under fire out in the field. The Staff Sergeant was so scared that he was talking gibberish. Even his crew couldn't understand what he was saying.

When we got back, and kind of situated, one of my crew

said, "Wow! Look at your flack jacket." The flack jacket was a cloth vest with fiberglass plates to stop shrapnel. Mine had two creases on the right side and one on the left from small arms fire. My experience in combat was that through good old USMC training you step up to the challenges and almost become oblivious to the incoming fire. You do what you have to do, and in combat you have to protect your men at all costs. You have a tradition you must live up to no matter what the cost to yourself. There were times when you were scared and times when you did not have any fear. I have experienced both. You could not let your men know that you were afraid. The times that I was the most frightened were when we were awakened in the middle of the night, or when I was drinking heavily, and we would get hit.

The gunner on the other tank was later MedEvaced out because of a wound to his knee. His knee started to get numb and he noticed a shrapnel wound. When the adrenaline is pumping so much, it is easy not to notice a wound until much later. Then it hurts like hell.

The pig was taken off of my tank to put wounded on, and I never saw it again. I couldn't help thinking that some Colonels and Generals were eating well that night.

That was not the only time I had a run in with that particular Staff Sergeant. Every night one person from each tank would take a two hour shift standing guard. Once, while the Staff Sergeant was with us, my relief woke me for my guard duty. I felt that I would lie there for a second longer, and I fell back to sleep. The Staff Sergeant woke me and was very pissed at me. I think he wanted to have me court marshalled. I think he tried everything he could do to get me for that incident. I didn't say anything at the time, but technically, it was the duty of the person who woke me to make sure I was awake and up before he went to sleep. The Staff Sergeant was rotated out soon after this incident. We had a long history of dislike for each other, but this one was our last encounter.

Back at the Mud Flats

The Staff Sergeant that I was not fond of was transferred to Hoi An, a city that had a multi-national hospital and the international store. We were not sorry to see him go. Our heavy section, or three tanks, sat guarding the gates to the city.

The Staff Sergeant was replaced by a Corporal in the mud flats and the ROK compound. I became the senior American. The ROK officers would invite me over to their bunker for dinner. It was there that I ate dried fish (tasted like toothpicks), octopus, and many other things that I never thought I would eat. I guess they thought that by sharing with me, I would protect them. I was not particularly fond of the food, but they were kind enough to share. It was their form of C rations. I preferred ours.

We went on several search and destroy missions during this time. The ROK Company Commander told me that he was going to put me in for a medal. After a short period of time, the ROK Company Commander called me to his bunker. He told me we were going on a week of missions. When morning came, we mounted up, started the engines, and did our communications check. We were ready. The ROK Marines were ready. I told my driver to back it out. He put it in reverse, but it would not go. The tank would go forward but not backward. I went to the driver's compartment and told him to get out. I jumped in and put it in reverse, and it would not go.

I called Company Headquarters. They put a mechanic on the radios. I explained the situation to him. He said that he would have to come out and look at it. The ROK Marines left for the search and destroy mission, eyeing us suspiciously as they passed. Later in the day a helicopter landed in our compound. It had supplies and our maintenance man. He said the transmission needed a new part. The helicopter came back and picked him up. The ROK Marines came back from the operation. They all gave me an evil glance, like it was my fault the tank was not working. Every day our maintenance man was flown back to Company Headquarters, and every morning they flew him back out. Finally, after a week, it was running again, just as the ROK Marines were coming back from an operation. I asked the commander if they had an operation the next day. He said, "Yes. I request one". The ROK Executive Officer later came up to me and said, "You should not have said that. That made the commander very mad." They had completed the operations by the time our tank was fixed. I guess I would have been pissed, too.

Once, when we returned from an operation, we had wounded ROK Marines. They had to be MedEvaced out. It was pitch dark by the time we got in. The MedEvac helicopter asked us to shine the tank search light to a place where he could set down. I had just been handed all the mail. I was sitting in the Tank Commander's hatch when he came in. I was directing the gunner where to shine the search light. We found the best, most level spot. Unfortunately, the pilot tried to land on the source of the light, not where we were trying to show him where to land. The helicopter was only about two feet above the tank before we waved him off and explained the situation. I was bent side ways, trying to prevent him from hitting me. I was close to jumping down inside the tank. The mail I had blew all over from the prop wash. We looked for the mail by flashlight that night. I am not sure if we ever found all of it. I felt bad because I knew we all really looked forward to getting news from the outside world.

After the helicopter pilot loaded up and started to lift off, the helicopter was hit in the hydraulic system by small arms fire and had to set back down. He came down hard and broke the right rear wheel. Another chopper came in and picked up the pilots, crew, and wounded. During the day, maintenance crews flew in to work on the chopper and were flown out in the evening. I often thought about the warm meals and cold beer that they were going back to. I was jealous.

After some time I was told I was going to Hoi An. A chopper came in. I got on, and he lifted off. I had no weapon except for a shoulder holster mounted forty five caliber pistol. I also had no hard helmet. When the chopper landed, it had about five grunts on board. I noticed all of them were sitting on their helmets. Soon we started to get incoming small arms fire, and I quickly realized why they were sitting on their helmets. It was hard to distinguish between the noise of the helicopter and the incoming rounds. I was thinking I sure wish I had a helmet to sit on. I cannot think of a worse place to get shot.

I arrived at Hoi An by jeep. It was so very different to be back in civilization or at least as close to it as I could get. It was very boring compared to the mud flats. All we did was sit in the tanks at the gates of the city in case of an attack. I was now in charge of the heavy section, or three tanks.

As I was sitting there I noticed a lovely woman walking across the street. She was close to six feet tall and very thin. She was wearing a white lab coat. She had long, pretty blond hair. I said to the guys, "Hey look at that." It was the first round-eye (a word used by us for a European woman) that I had seen in almost a year.

They said, "Yeah, she is a nurse at the hospital." I waited every day after that to see her. She was very beautiful. I saw her from a half a block away, and she occupied my mind for days. I was told she was a German nurse. I felt that with all of the important people she sees, she would not appreciate a lowly Marine trying to strike up a conversation with her, so I never bothered to get close to her.

I got a call on the radios. A jeep came to pick me up, and I was loaded on a helicopter to return to the mud flats. The Corporal had taken my bunker so I had to move to the bunker on the other end of the compound. It soon became rickety and had to be repaired. I decided that since we had plenty of time, we should build a new one. We started to dig in the berm of highway four. We never got to finish it.

We went on many operations with the ROK Marines. During one particular operation, the two tanks were traveling through a large field of low grass. The tanks were side by side about two hundred feet apart with the ROK Marines spread out in between and flanking on each side. It looked like a photo of what a military operation should look like on a perfect day. It was a nice, warm, comfortable day. It was about 80 degrees, which is comfortable for that area. We started to take sniper fire. The ROK Marines ran up to the tanks and tried to get as close as possible. I was not concerned in the least. The rounds were not close to us. They were way over our heads. I had no idea where the rounds originated from, so to fire back would have been a shot in the dark, literally.

We moved on. Soon, one of the tanks threw a track. The other tank was commanded by a Corporal, and now I was in the hot seat since I was the highest ranking non-commissioned officer. The large track keeper (center guide) on the center of the track slipped out from in between a double set of road wheels. Usually this happened when a driver turned the tank while it was in a rut or against a small hill.

We tried to walk it back on by steering the tank in the opposite direction and driving ahead. If this failed, we had to break the track and move it back on by hand with crow bars and track jacks, which was the case. While we were struggling with the track, Company Headquarters called on the radios. They wanted to know what our position was and what we were doing. I told the loader who was monitoring the radios to tell them that I would call them back when I got a chance. I am sure they did not like that response. We were so far removed from our Company Headquarters for so long that we became a little independent. We were pretty much on our own and did not feel the need to report to them for every little detail of what we were doing.

Sometimes we would sustain minor wounds and were treated by the Korean Corpsman or by ourselves. Paint chips were a common injury. A round would hit the tank and splatter paint off the tank. This would hit you in the face or hands causing a small wound. The chips were about half an inch or smaller, but with the force behind them, they could easily break the skin. If we had more serious injuries, we would radio for a MedEvac helicopter.

Once a week we were resupplied by helicopter. We would receive one case of warm beer (usually Budweiser), C rations from WWII, mail, and ammo. If we opened a beer right away half of it was gone in foam. We would have to wait for about an hour. We got so used to drinking warm beer, that once we had a cold beer again, it did not taste right at first. The wounded and transfers were sent out on the supply helicopter. It was usually carried in on a CH46, or grasshopper as I thought of them.

As we finished with the track, the other Tank Commander and I stopped to thank each other for the help and wipe the dirt and sweat from our faces. We heard a very loud crack right between us. The sniper found us and hit a road wheel located right between the Corporal and myself. The sound was magnified by the drum shape of the road wheel. We examined the impact area. We both smiled and I said, "I guess we better mount up." This was a common experience for us, so it was not alarming. Surely the sniper had his range, and the next shot would have found its mark.

As we started to move on, I called Headquarters back. They were very upset with me for not reporting the track throwing incident to them when they first called.

We were in a small compound living in bunkers with all kinds of bugs. The bunkers were dug down in the ground, then lined with sandbags. The sandbags came up to about five feet high. There was just enough room to fit four cots in it. The roof was about three layers of sandbags. We had to walk down a ramp to get into the bunker, and duck at the bottom. There were no windows, so the only light we had was from the entrance way. There was no door. There were huge thousand-leggers (centipedes) in this area, and I was told that they were poisonous. The nasty suckers were about eight inches long. They would not kill you but could make you very sick. As I was lying in my cot I felt something on my chest. I saw a huge thousand-legger walking on me. I said, "Shit, look at this!"

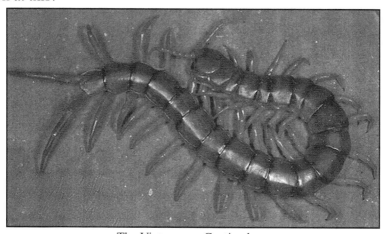

The Vietnamese Centipede

I thought of taking my forty five and trying to shoot it off of my chest, but you can imagine where that might have gotten me. Immediately one of the guys said, "Don't hit it! Wait until it's off of you. If you kill it while it's on you, it will bite you." I never saw one of these critters before, and I was not too happy while I waited for it to finish its journey across me. It seemed like an hour but was probably closer to three minutes. I hear that some people have these things as pets now!

We were on a routine search and destroy operation. There was an explosion on the left side of my tank. I thought it was a rocket propelled grenade and thought an attack was eminent. I opened up in the nearby jungle with the fifty caliber machine gun. After a few good bursts, I realized it was kind of quiet. There was no incoming. The ROK Marines searched the area and found an antipersonnel mine, which was planted to hurt or maim the enemy. One of my crew told me that I was bleeding. I had a gash in my wrist and blood running to my elbow. I had shrapnel from the mine stuck under my skin. I did not even feel it until it was all over. You have to love adrenaline. I was treated by an ROK Corpsman. He pulled the shrapnel out, put antiseptic on it, and bandaged it. Had I been treated by an American Corpsman, I would have been put in for a Purple Heart. Since I was treated by a Korean Corpsman, I never received one.

Incidents like this one were seldom reported to the Company Headquarters. The only way they knew about them was if you got MedEvaced out. At first it kind of bothered me, then I thought, "How many guys have you seen that were injured badly and all they got was a Purple Heart. This was a minor wound." However, we had people in the rear who hardly ever saw any action but received a Purple Heart. One I remember was a Lieutenant who ran out of the officer's club hootch and ran into a pole. I heard he got a Purple Heart for that. He probably ran for office later in life.

We were three quarters of the way finished with the bunker that we were building when I was told by radio to get everything in order. We were to head west through the brush, with the two tanks and all our belongings, until we came to a road. From there we traveled to C Company Headquarters.

I learned much later that the replacement tankers were upset because we did not wait for them to tell them what was going on. I did not know that there were replacements on the way. I just followed orders.

Some of the guys felt a need for advice on so many different matters. It amazed me. Some of them asked advice on their girlfriends or what they should write their parents about Vietnam. One guy asked me if he should stay in the military. I felt that it was my duty as the senior ranking American, when I was the senior ranking person, to answer their questions in the best way that I could. When I was not the senior person the guys came to me anyway. I guess they felt more comfortable with me than the other Sergeants or officers.

At night, when it was quiet, I would lay there thinking about it. I thought to myself, what the hell do I know? I gave the best advice I could, but really, how did I know any better than they did? To some of these guys, it was like you were their parent. To some of them, you were more like a parent than they had ever had. I felt like a minister at times.

I was twenty one and was responsible for two to three tanks and eight to twelve people, seven days a week, twenty four hours a day, in high stress, combat situations. It was really a lot of responsibility for someone that age.

Cau Do River Bridge

Highway One ran south from Da Nang. It was, for the most part, cinders and stone patchwork due to the destruction of mines and bombs. It was wide enough for troops and civilians to walk along the sides as military vehicles drove down the center. There was a constant flow of people going to and from Da Nang. Most walked, but some traveled by Mopeds. The Mopeds usually had a whole family as well as supplies stacked on them. I only saw two cars in my time in Vietnam. One tried to cut in front of a tank, and the whole front of it was crushed.

It amazed me to watch these people. You would see people with a six foot pole over their shoulders and baskets of goods on each end of the pole. Most of these people weighed one hundred pounds at the most. I don't think I could have carried all they did for such a distance, and I was in pretty good shape! Some of the guys would open the door of their truck, put their foot behind it, and let it hit the people walking on the highway, knocking them off the road. I didn't understand what they got out of doing that.

Intersecting highway one was a river called the Cau Do River. The bridge crossing the river was the Cau Do River Bridge. The enemy was constantly trying to blow up the bridge so two tanks or a light section would guard it. The bridge was old, and it reminded me of the old rail road bridge back home. It was wide enough for one tank to cross at a time. If there were people on the bridge, they would have to stand off to the side to let the tank pass.

At the bridge, the river was wide, slow, and very dark. There were low grasses along the edge. I really didn't know if the river was dark from mud or so many minerals from the jungles it wound through.

We were sent to guard the bridge. On the side toward Da Nang, the tank sat on a small rise and had a great view. The spot on the other side of the river was cut out by a blade tank. There was a slot wide enough to drive a tank into. When a tank was parked in the slot, only the turret was visible. We could walk up to and step on the fenders without having to climb up the wheels.

If we were attacked, it would have been at the south side of the bridge. The south side was closest to the jungle, which provided protection for the enemy. That is why I chose the south side.

Soon after we settled in, the children showed up. I had to get used to the little guys again. They were in our hooch. I did not let them on or near the tanks.

We sat there for about three weeks guarding the bridge. Sometimes grunts would show up for a few days. It was actually a very peaceful time for us. It was very enjoyable to sit on the tank and just watch the world around us going on like a performance.

Every evening the children would bring the water buffalo down to the river for a swim. It was amazing to see such small children control these huge animals. Sometimes there would be up to eight water buffalo and eight children at a time. The buffalo would group together, and the children used them much like we would use a raft or pier. They would jump and dive off of the buffalo. It was very entertaining to watch.

I once saw a buffalo chase a squad of grunts around a field. They shot it many times before it finally dropped. The animals would tolerate the children but would snort and threaten any American. One charged a tank I was in once. I told the driver to stop so we could see what would happen. The buffalo got very close to the tank and at the last second turned and ran away. I guess it did not perceive us as a threat.

Two days after we were told to leave the bridge, I got word that it was almost overrun. A gunner was killed when an RPG penetrated the tank and went through his chest. I believed God was looking out for me.

We sat on guard duty at another bridge (I forget the name) for a week or so. The grunts used C-4 to set off charges to foil divers that may attempt to blow the bridge up. I watched the grunts with C-4 so much they finally asked if I wanted to do it. I said, "Sure" as casually as I could, although I was really excited. I became an authority on C-4 in our platoon. I was always asked to set the charge when needed, like when there was a tree stump in our football field or a stubborn torsion bar that refused to come out. (A torsion bar was a steel bar about six feet long that attached to the road wheels and anchored in the belly of the hull of the tank.

They would break if we hit a ditch the wrong way.) It was at this bridge that we learned C-4 was great for heating C rations. If it had a blasting cap, it would detonate. If it was lit by fire it would burn very quickly.

Next we were sent to a compound on the north side of Da Nang. We seldom ventured north of the city, because we had to go through Da Nang with the tanks and we had never done that before. We were used to traveling at a very fast rate of speed depending on the terrain. The only time we went slowly was when we were with grunts and needed to stay with them.

A Lieutenant was with us, and he sat on the loader's hatch. I was in the Tank Commander's hatch. As we were traveling through the city we were soaking up the sights. Soon someone realized that a jeep with two MP's (Military Police) was trying to get us to stop. The lieutenant told the driver to stop. He climbed down to see what they wanted. They told him that we were speeding. I remained emotionless on the outside but on the inside was hysterically laughing. I had to work to control myself. I kept thinking, "Just what the hell would they do if we didn't stop?" Would they shoot us with their 45's? Would we get a traffic ticket? Thank God the Lieutenant took care of this or I would have certainly gotten myself in trouble.

When we arrived at the compound, what struck me the most was that it had a ten foot tall gate. I never saw one so high before! After we settled in, one of the grunts came over and started a conversation with me. We talked for some time when he mentioned, "We are going to sneak a girl into the compound tonight. You are more than welcome to join in."

I said, "No thanks!" I was never into the group thing.

The next morning I asked him how it went. He said, "Great! Eleven guys had their fun, and then we threw her out without paying her." I didn't say anything, but I was glad I had nothing to do with it. She was probably trying to help support a family or her parents, and these guys completely screwed her. It was not because they didn't have the money. We usually had so much money that we had no idea where to spend it. At times like this, I wondered why the Vietnamese people helped the north.

Once while supporting the Korean Marines, I was sleeping on the ground. I took my watch off and put it right beside my head. In the morning it was gone. After I got a new watch, I decided to set a trap for the Korean crook. I took my watch off, put it beside me, and took out an incendiary grenade. I pulled the pin. As I attempted to attach it to my watch, the spoon slipped, and it went off in my hand. I immediately threw the grenade. It burnt my hand very badly. I tried to sleep. The next day went to a Korean Corpsman. The inside of my hand was a big blister bubble. The Corpsman cut all the skin off the palm of my hand and my fingers and put a salve on it. I was amazed at how fast it had healed. The night it happened, I was worried about ligament damage, but there was none.

Cau Do River Bridge
Courtesy of Ralph Schwartz

An ISO Show. This was our entertainment in Viet Nam, courtesy of
the United States. The guys in the rear got Bob Hope.
Courtesy of David Forsyth

Drugs in Vietnam

Let's take a moment to discuss a topic that was all the rage during the time period. I have heard all kinds of stories about drugs in Vietnam. Unless I was naive, they were not very prevalent. I know some of the guys smoked pot. They would sit on the radios at night in safe places and talk to different outfits. It was so easy for them to get it from civilians, and very cheap. I can honestly say I never tried any drugs while in Vietnam. I felt I had to set a good example, and I had enough problems without drugs. Usually drug issues were taken care of by the noncoms or Non Commissioned Officers in our own way. Sometimes it was a whack up side the head, a very good ass chewing, or both.

I told the guys in my group that if they smoked pot, they had better not do it while on guard duty. I told them I would burn them (bring them up on charges) if I caught them smoking while on guard duty. I was easy-going with the guys, because of the situation we were in, but that is one thing I would not tolerate.

One of the guys told me once when we were sitting on the perimeter berm of the compound at the South China Sea, "I need to smoke once in a while because it clears my mind". I told him,"What I don't see, I can't do anything about, but you better not smoke that shit while on guard duty." Clears his mind. The only thing the drugs will do is let you forget where you are for a short while. It may also get you killed.

Our Communications Sergeant told me that the Company Headquarters was almost overrun. The North Vietnamese smelled the grunts on guard duty smoking pot and used that location to launch their attack. They almost succeeded.

Alcohol was a different matter. Beer was everywhere and cheap. My policy on beer was no drinking on duty. This was a much later time and much different place than when we were drinking wine on the mountain. Sometimes someone would have to run to Hoi An, a city quite a ways to our south. There was an international store there where we could purchase hard stuff. I got several bottles of Johnny Walker during my stay in Vietnam. Oddly enough, I did not go to the store when I was there as heavy section leader in charge of three tanks. It was so very different when I was responsible for the tanks and men that manned them. I was all serious then. When someone else was in charge I could relax and be myself. Alcohol always depended on the situation and the circumstances.

There is no difference in drug usage between Vietnam Veterans and non-Vietnam Veterans of the same age group.

Communications Sergeant

Our Communications Sergeant's job was to keep our radios working and to man the communications and command bunker when the company headquarters was under attack.

When I was sent out in the field from Company Headquarters I had the best location for my rack that was possible. It was in the back portion of the Sergeant's quarters. There was a nice cot, and the quarters were sectioned off so that I shared this section with one other Sergeant. As soon as I left, the Communications Sergeant claimed it. He even got a refrigerator. I have no idea where or how he got it.

Once when he had com watch, or monitoring the company radios in the communications and command bunker, he said they were having a cookout at the mess hall and would I pick him up some chicken. I said sure and stopped at the enlisted men's club for a quick beer. I told the guys that I was drinking with that I had to get some chicken for the Communications Sergeant. They said to have another beer first. Soon I forgot all about him. The next day he was so mad at me that he would not talk to me.

Soon after I rotated out, he ran amuck. He asked the Company Commander for his own jeep. The CO said, "Hell no!"

The Communications Sergeant said, "I will steal one from the Army."

The CO said, "I don't want to hear about it." He did steal a jeep from the Army, then painted it and numbered it to look exactly like our company jeep. He just walked into the Army motor pool, picked one out, started it up, and drove away. He said he just tried to look official and confident. This is the guy that I knew would be successful in life, because he was a great communicator. He could talk his way into and out of anything. He ended up being a high school principal.

Communication Sergeant and Village Children
Courtesy of Gary Mefford

Stolen Army Jeep
Courtesy of Gary Mefford

Gary and Clyde
Courtesy of Gary Mefford

Marble Mountain

C Company Headquarters was a few miles south of Marble Mountain. Marble Mountain was a huge, HUGE porous rock at the end of the MSR (military service road). We shared the compound with a company of grunts. First it was 2/26, later it was 2/1. Sometimes a platoon of Am Trks were stationed there. Company Headquarters was a fairly safe place to me. We would get occasional sniper fire and mortar attacks, but, as I said before, the North Vietnamese were poor shots. With all the sniper fire I remember, and it was a lot, I can only recall one person getting hit.

Marble Mountain

I received a package from my girlfriend back home. In it was an audio tape. One of the guys had a player so I asked him if I could use it. Unfortunately, it was in a hooch with a lot of the guys. I played a part of it until it got too personal. She was talking about how much she missed me and some of the stuff we used to do. I shut it off, thinking about playing it when I had some privacy. I stored it in my sea bag where all my possessions were stored, except for my shaving gear and a few sets of clothes. It was in the company storage hooch. I was sent out to one of the hottest places in enemy territory. I thought it was very ironic when I received a radio call saying that the hootch containing my sea bag was destroyed by an enemy rocket. Almost all of my earthly possessions had literally gone up in smoke. I felt that the company area was one of the most secure areas. I guess you were never totally safe, no matter where you were.

Hootch Destroyed by Enemy Rockets.
All of my earthly belongings were destroyed in this attack.
Courtesy of David Forsyth

We were to assist a platoon of grunts on a small operation very close to Company Headquarters. There were three tanks, and luckily we had a Lieutenant with us. I say "luckily" because when we had a Lieutenant with us, I was no longer the highest ranking person. It took a lot of pressure off of me. The grunts destroyed some bunkers. Not much else happened, so we set up a small encampment for the night in the middle of a large field of low grass. We talked to and made friends with some of the grunts. They climbed up on the turret and sat with us. The grunts were always eager to learn about tanks, but in combat they always kept their distance from us.

Late at night, there was an explosion overhead followed by many more. There were explosions everywhere. You could feel the concussion with each explosion. They were about ten or twenty feet over our heads. You could see the sparks and fire fly from each burst. The artillery rounds were very close to us.

Not knowing what was going on around us, the tankers jumped inside the tank, along with about eight grunts. The tank is made for a crew of four which is a tight fit, but to have four tankers and eight grunts in a tank is like all the clowns squeezed into a small car at a circus. We were squashed in there. That was one of the only times I can remember closing all the hatches. It was so hot and stuffy with all of us crammed in there. That was the only time I ever saw grunts jump inside of a tank for protection. The rest of the grunts were all trying to keep as close to the tank as possible for protection.

I heard the Lieutenant calling on the radios to let Company Headquarters know that we were under attack. That is when we found out that it was our own one hundred five millimeter artillery. We withstood a large aerial artillery barrage.

I was very concerned that if there was an attack, how would I get the grunts out so we could do our job. I do not think that they would have been very happy if I had told them to get out. Soon after the explosions stopped, I opened the Tank Commander's hatch to see what had happened. We all came out to look around. There were grunts squeezed under and around the tanks. Remarkably there were very few wounded and none killed.

Later, I asked how something like this could happen. I was told the North Vietnamese had someone who spoke English very well. They had someone monitor our radios for weeks to pick up our call signs. When they figured them out, the English speaking person called them in for a barrage. I saw this happen to a friendly village near C Company Compound. The civilians brought in many killed or wounded men, women, and children. It was a very sad sight.

I was told that I was going to attend a briefing for another operation. When the time neared, a jeep picked me up and away we went. I was not sure where it was, but the driver knew. We arrived at a large steel building with no windows. The driver made himself comfortable in the jeep as I headed for the building.

As I approached, I was ushered inside and to a seat. I sat down and looked around. I was very surprised that I did not see any enlisted men. All that were attending were Generals, Colonels, and a few Lieutenants. Most of them were Generals of various branches and countries. I had never seen so much brass at one spot in my life. I was sure I was the only one in the room that spent time in the field. They all wore rank insignia, and I did not.

A Korean private asked if I would like some coffee. I said, "Sure." I was surprised to be handed a tall glass of iced coffee, my first ever. I had never even heard of it before.

I felt kind of cocky with all the brass but also a little humble. I felt that if I spoke, they would realize that an uneducated person was in their midst. The meeting was to talk about how we were some type of blocking force to prevent the enemy from getting away. On my part, the operation was uneventful.

Hygiene! We were excellent at bathing in a helmet. A helmet was also good for cooking. We would sometimes take several types of C rations and combine them in a helmet to cook over a fire. It was a feast. We could shave and bathe in a helmet full of water. On operations we would sometimes come to rivers or large bomb craters that filled up with water. Both, if safe, made for good bathing. The large bomb craters from the USS New Jersey or five hundred pound bombs made large swimming pools.

Once, a grunt stepping out of a river after bathing, stepped on something. After examination they found several two hundred twenty millimeter rockets. They must have been stored there by the North Vietnamese to be used later on against us. The grunts detonated them.

Water at Company Headquarters was supplied by a large water container, which we called a water buffalo. It contained about five hundred gallons. Halizone Tablets were used to purify the water. Also, back at Company Headquarters, we had a shower. It was a large airplane fuel tank filled with water. The water would warm by the day so we had warm showers in the evening. It was great to be there.

It was so hot and humid that when the cool weather came, we were freezing. I remember being told it was one hundred twenty seven degrees. So when it got down to around sixty degrees, it was very cold to us. A cold shower at this time was very unpleasant but necessary.

When the monsoon season neared, we were called back to Company Headquarters. I was unhappy about it. I did not like going back there, even though they had the warm showers. When I was there I was just one of many Sergeants. However, when the rains started I was happy to be there. I never saw rain like that before. It would rain for days and so hard that you could not see more than ten feet in front of you.

It was a damp, cold, miserable time; but it would have been much more miserable had we still been out in the field. Nothing was dry. Everything felt wet and uncomfortable. Everything was always wet over there, either from sweat or very high humidity, even when the monsoons were not going on.

We had walkways from hootch to hootch so you would not get stuck in the mud. It was a very depressing time. We played cards and drank beer most of the time.

Grunts Leaving Charlie Co Headquarters During a Break in the Monsoon.
Courtesy of Gary Mefford

By now my memory is blurred on some operations. Some I remember with crystal clarity. I can still remember some of the conversations I had with people. There were so many ambushes and shoot outs. I do not remember them all.

I remember one incident where, for some reason, I climbed

on the back of another tank just as it was about to fire the main gun. I was not wearing a helmet or hearing protection. No one ever mentioned hearing protection. Besides we were Marines, not sissies. When thc main gun fired, it stunned me. I felt like I was hit along side the head with a two by four- not a good feeling. I made sure this never happened again. Almost every tanker I know has hearing problems now, including myself.

At Company Headquarters, we were getting the tanks ready for another operation. We started to hear a strange noise coming from the jungle. It was such a weird, loud noise. It sounded like hundreds of women crying and screaming at the same time. Some of the guys walked to the front gate to see what was going on.

Soon, Vietnamese people started to appear through the jungle. They were crying and wailing together, and it made an inhumane noise. They were carrying wounded and dying men, women, and children. It was a horrible sight.

Apparently a Marine artillery unit fired a barrage onto their village. The village was south of us and the artillery rounds passed close to us. Having been so familiar with the sound of artillery, we did not even pay attention to it.

I had no idea where the village was located or how far the people came. It was a sight that I will always see in my mind with crystal clarity. All of those little children - some dead, some dying. Seeing women and children mutilated by war is something that I cannot ever forget. These Vietnamese people were carrying their own dead and wounded children, wives, husbands, and grandchildren. It put a knot in my stomach. They walked past us, not even looking at us, crying and wailing. We watched until they were out of sight behind the hootches. They walked to our small, makeshift sickbay to be treated by the Corpsmen. I did not go to help them, as I was not very good at that sort of thing. I went back to working on the tanks, but the images stayed with me. I was solemn for the rest of the day.

Navy Corpsman. Unless you are a Marine you probably do not know that the Marine Corps does not have their own Corpsman. They have Navy personnel trained to work with Marines. Now, there has always been an ongoing conflict between the Navy and Marine Corps, although, technically, the Marine Corps is under the jurisdiction of the Navy. In boot camp, the drill instructors condemned the Navy, so we were basically trained to dislike them. Although the Corpsmen were Navy, they were quite respected by the Marines. After all, they could save your life. They traveled with the grunts, and did everything the same way as the grunts, they just did not shoot. I once told our Corpsman that I think it was a lot easier to pull a trigger than it was to try to patch up a wounded, or possibly dying person.

One thing that amazed me was the amount of wounded and killed from that artillery barrage on the Vietnamese village. The artillery barrage that I was in had a few wounded and no dead. I could not rationalize how this could be. How could this be so? The only thing I could think of is that as Marines, we are trained to hit the dirt. These civilians must have been running around, screaming, and not knowing what to do. So sad. I felt uncomfortable seeing women or children killed. It was one thing for men, but women and children made me feel worse. Women and children should not be involved in war.

*"When Elephants fight,
it's the grass that suffers."
-African Proverb*

A Visitor

I was coming back to Company Headquarters from a three day operation. I made sure the tanks were secure. I went to the hootch that I was living in and started to store my gear. I took the magazine from my forty five caliber pistol that all tankers carried in a shoulder holster.

I thought about the incident we had weeks before where someone hung their shoulder holster on a hook, but he had not removed the magazine or taken the round out of the chamber. It slipped off the hanger, hit the floor, and fired, killing another one of the guys in our platoon. No charges were filed and the incident went down as KIA or killed in action.

I could not wait to take a shower, eat, and have a few beers at the enlisted men's club. Someone walked into the hootch and interrupted my thoughts. He said, "Someone was here to visit you."

I thought to myself, "Who the hell would visit me here?" I said, "Who was it, and what did he want?" He told me that he said he was a friend of mine and that he was in an Army uniform. My mind raced. Who do I know in Vietnam in the Army? It dawned on me that a childhood friend was here in Vietnam and in the Army. How could he find me over here, I thought? He must have gone way out of his way to find me.

He and I were very young when we started to hang out together. Probably five or six years old. He lived four houses down the street. We were always together, we walked to school together. He was one grade lower than I was, but we waited for each other and instead of taking the bus, we walked to school. We played Army with the other kids in the neighborhood all the time. He was much more timid than I was. He was a good person.

I was so sorry I missed him. It would have been great to have a beer or two with him at the club. I thought about how I could contact him. I had no idea. I did not even know what outfit he was in.

I thought about writing home to ask them if they could find out for me. I seldom wrote home. What can you say? It was hot as hell and just as humid. The mosquitoes were really bad last night?

I almost bought it today? I wish I was home! I never got around to writing home and asking about him.

About a month later I received a newspaper article in the mail from my family. He was KIA or killed in action over here. I could not believe it. Why him? Why not me instead? After all he was a better person than I was. It was just not fair. Why the hell are we even here? Why the hell do so many have to die and for what?

He was awarded the Silver Star - a big price to pay for a fourteen dollar medal. There was a saying in the military at the time - twenty five cents and a medal will get you a cup of coffee. At the time coffee was twenty five cents. I could not even make his funeral.

While I was home on leave from the Med cruise, I ran into two friends with whom I hung out quite a bit until I went into the service. I told them both that it was great in the Marine Corps. I told them that I was on a Med cruise where there was plenty of alcohol and women. After boot camp and ITR, it was like a regular job, except you had guard duty once in a while.

Both enlisted in the Marines, both went to Vietnam, and neither one ever went on a Med cruise. One was killed accidentally. I felt very responsible for his death.

Another death that bothered me was someone who came into the tanks at the same time I did. Actually four of us came into tanks at the same time, so we naturally hung out together. We were the same rank and the same age. He was one of the nicest people you could ever meet. He came from Kentucky and every time someone asked him where he was from he said, "Tucky". I was told an RPG came through the side of his tank and hit a white phosphorus round on the inside. When it exploded it sent burning white phosphorous spewing around inside the tank. I was told he could not be MedEvaced out that night because of heavy fighting. He died of severe burns beside his tank. I felt great sorrow and anger for all three deaths. They were all very special people - their lives taken away before they ever really grew up. What a pity. What a price our country had asked of us.

Military Payment Certificate

We were paid with MPC (military payment certificate) or as we called it funny money. Instead of using American money, or Vietnamese money, the Military made up their own currency. The military did not want us dealing with the local people, and this was their way of controlling the flow of money.

The Marine Corps did not like us to keep wallets because they did not want the lump in our back pockets. We used to carry our money in our socks because it was much harder to lose or get pick-pocketed.

One time, we were all rounded up and taken by truck to Da Nang. We went to a large building surrounded by concertina wire. Nobody had any idea what was going on. It was top secret. Once inside, we were told to turn in all of our current MPC and exchange it for a new MPC. It meant nothing to us, but it was devastating to the Vietnamese in the black market and others who found a way to get the MPC. Everything they had was worthless. I remember seeing a prostitute crying at the gate. She had a huge bundle of the old MPC in her hand. She might as well have been holding blank papers.

Military Payment Certificate
Photo Courtesy of Ralph Schwartz

The Mine

It was time for another small operation with the grunts. We were sent on so many operations, and we did not even know the names of most of them. We just met the grunt Commanding Officer, got a short run down, and we were on our way. On one such incident, we had a new Lieutenant with us. Seldom were officers out in the bush with us. I thought of Vietnam as a Sergeant's war.

We headed out with the grunts flanking us. We were somewhere south of our Company Headquarters, which was south of Marble Mountain, probably twenty miles south of Da Nang. After a couple of uneventful hours we stopped and waited, probably for the Commanding Officer of the operation to coordinate the complete operation. We were just a small piece of the pie.

Soon we received the word to head back. No combat - this was great. The Lieutenant on my tank was new in the country. I had been there a while, so he pretty much let me do what I wanted. I asked the grunt Commander if his men would like a ride back. We had two tanks on this operation and only a couple of squads of grunts, so, there was room for the grunts to ride. As they mounted up, I asked the grunt Commander to make sure the men had their feet on top of the tank fenders. It did offer some protection if we hit a mine. He did not pass this information on to his men. I should have stopped and ordered him to do so; however, I did not want to get into an argument with a grunt officer.

As we drove back, I told the driver to half track the previous tracks. It was customary to follow your exact same track back from an operation. The Viet Cong would sometimes take advantage of this and very carefully plant a mine in the same tracks so you hit it when you came back. To half track the old track, you simply had one track in between the old track marks left on the ground.

We were all relaxed and happy to be going back. It was a warm but not too exceptionally hot day. I was sitting on the Tank Commander's hatch, and the Lieutenant was sitting on the loader's hatch as we headed back to Company Headquarters. Even with a fiberglass tank helmet, the noise from the track can be very loud.

Then I had another of the two weirdest experiences I ever

had in my life. I took a very deep breath of air. It was so hot that it scalded my throat. Everything started to get fuzzy and dark. I thought, "Oh Hell! This is it." I have no idea how long I was unconscious. I did not fall through the hatch inside the tank, as far as I know. I do not remember taking my tank helmet off. One minute I was happy, relaxed, and content. The next minute it was deathly quiet and everything seemed unreal. I was missing time in between.

It was quiet when I started to see some small light, even though it was all very fuzzy. It took some time for me to focus. It was like looking at the world through the bottom of a drinking glass. I do not remember hearing the explosion at all. At this point I was very confused and disoriented. I looked around and there were some wounded grunts on the ground.

What had happened? I was trying to figure out what was going on. It took quite some time for me to realize that we had hit a mine. If we hit a mine, why didn't I hear or see the explosion? It was on the same side of the tank where I was sitting. Why was it so very quiet now? Why did everything seem so unreal?

I saw the Lieutenant on the ground. I saw mouths moving but I didn't hear any words. I thought that I should do something, but what could I do? I did not know. I needed to attend to the wounded. After all, this was entirely my fault. I should not have gone back the exact same way. The wounded were being taken care of. What could I do? The Lieutenant told me much later that one of the grunts said he was going to kill the Lieutenant for getting him wounded. I didn't hear this conversation or any others for quite some time.

I had heard later that a piece of rubber from the track entered through one grunt's heel and exited out his knee. Another had a bunch of small pieces of metal in his head.

Three road wheels (the wheels that roll on the top of the lower part of the track.) were missing and the tank tilted into a large hole in the ground probably eight feet round and two to three feet deep. I heard someone say with authority that it was about thirty pounds of explosives.

We were not too far from a dirt road; and after about an

hour, my Company Commander showed up in a jeep along with a tank and two maintenance men. The maintenance men started to shorten the track so it would drive by the sprocket and just not have all the road wheels. As we returned to our Company Headquarters, the driver of my tank had to keep steering to the left to compensate for the short track.

While maintenance was busy with the track, my Company Commander gave the Lieutenant and me a really, really good ass chewing. He felt we should have known better than to travel back the same way we travelled before. This was the route the grunts had wanted us to use. This lecture lasted for about ten minutes. Unfortunately, my hearing had somewhat returned for it. I really felt bad for the Lieutenant, as it was all my call and entirely my fault. I never told him, but to this day, I regret that whole mess. I never knew what happened with the wounded grunts. They were trucked away, and I never saw them again.

As far as I know, the driver and I were the only ones that were knocked unconscious. No one bothered to ask if we were okay! I felt disoriented for about a week after this incident.

My tank sat in our company tank park for months. I had this memento to look at for a long time. I had the great pleasure of being sent out on many other tanks while mine was waiting on parts. It was like driving a rental car instead of your own.

We lost a Lieutenant to a sniper a few months after this incident. I believe it was the same Lieutenant. He had a flack jacket on and raised his arm. A round hit him in the arm pit and killed him. I was not on this operation with him at the time.

We were issued Flack Jackets, which were a nylon vest with ballistic nylon plates on the inside. They were made to prevent soldiers from getting injured by fragments of shrapnel. They would not stop a round but would slow it down. They were incredibly hot to wear in such a humid environment.

Most tankers seldom wore the Flack Jackets, except when they were in an extremely hostile area. They restricted the tankers from climbing inside or outside of the tank. While inside the tank, they were hardly ever used. If the tank armor did not stop something, the jacket certainly was not going to help! Those of us who were exposed on top of the tank sometimes wore them but hardly ever closed the front of them. It was better air circulation. Several times I saw the Flack Jacket prevent wounds.

Tank that hit a mine.
Photo courtesy of Gary Mefford

The Leper Colony

I was back at Charlie Company Headquarters. I had gotten word we were to move out in a couple of hours. Time to give the tank and ammo situation a good check and to get our personal gear together. We carried very little personal gear. The C rations were pretty much self contained. We all carried a P-38, or small can opener. C rations were cooked with a little heat tab that was furnished or C-4, the explosive. With a small amount of C-4, you could cook a can of C rations in seconds. C-4 was highly explosive if ignited with a blasting cap; but if it was lit with a match, it burned very fast. A case of C rations were usually sufficient for most operations. Some guys carried a P-38 on a chain around their neck with their dog tags.

We sometimes carried a poncho liner. It was very light and warm. If you wrapped it around you, it was usually all you needed for a good night's sleep. Finding a place to sleep was a different matter. I set up rules on my tank so that we rotated where we slept every night to be fair to all. One person slept inside the turret, one on the engine plate, and two on the ground. The person in the turret was the most comfortable and the most protected. I remember one rainy night, when it was my turn on the ground, I slept in at least three inches of water. It was about mid-shoulder when I was lying down on my back. What a long night it was. It was raining hard, and I was laying in it.

All of our personal gear - poncho, shaving gear, etc. - was placed in fifty caliber ammo boxes and placed on the racks on the back of the turret. Once I bought an eight mm movie camera from a guy. I kept it in a fifty caliber ammo box to keep it dry. I had movies of air strikes. I could have gotten in a lot of trouble for shooting the movie instead of shooting the guns. I gave a whole bunch of movies to a maintenance guy to send back for me. We were not allowed to do this, but if the movies were wrapped in aluminum foil, they would not show up on the X-ray. I never saw the movies again. I think he kept them with him or mailed them to his own house. I wonder if he made a lot of money off of them.

The grunts had to carry everything they needed on their

backs including ammo. They sometimes had wet feet for so long that they developed jungle rot. The skin would start to deteriorate and peel off. We carried water in five gallon cans (sometimes two to three) on the bustle rack on the back of the turret. We usually shared this water with the grunts on operations.

During breaks in action, the grunts would sometimes climb up on the tank to check it out. A few said we were lucky. Some said, "I wouldn't want nothing to do with this tracked coffin." When rough times came, no one cared about a grunt with a rifle - everyone concentrated on the big stuff. We were like a magnet for all kinds of weapons. We were also called out when grunts were pinned down or expecting adverse enemy activity. Sometimes we would return from one operation only to be immediately sent out on another.

We mounted up mid afternoon. There were three tanks on this operation, and a Lieutenant was with us. There was a company of American Marine grunts in a compound near a leper colony just south of Da Nang. The grunts were almost overrun by the North Vietnamese Army the night before, so they asked for reinforcements.

We drove up the beach. The South China Sea was beautiful and peaceful. Soon we came across some hootches about two hundred feet from the shore. This is another sight, from my Vietnam experience, that I will never forget. It was a leper colony. I read about leprosy in school, but you just cannot grasp it until you have seen it for yourself. Some of the people were in the water, and some were near the hootches. I guess the water helped ease the pain. We drove through the middle of them. I saw people missing noses, ears, legs, arms. Some of the faces were so disfigured that it was hard to tell that they were human, let alone male or female. Where these appendages once were, now there were just blotchy red spots of meat. There were men, women, and children, just like a regular village, except they were all deformed from the disease. It may have been an irrational fear, but I was afraid we might catch it. I was terrified, actually. At the time, we did not know where Leprosy came from or what caused it. To my knowledge, there was no cure. They stared at us as we went by, and we stared at them. Not one person on the tanks said a word. It was a terribly shocking experience. I remembering wondering why God chose to torture these people like this.

Soon we neared the small compound ringed with concertina wire. The wire was made to slow the enemy down in case of an attack. The wire was only thirty feet from the jungle, and the tanks were only twenty feet from the wire. This is a very close range for rocket propelled grenades or snipers. The jungle was very dense. I was uncomfortable with the closeness of the tanks to the jungle. At night the enemy could be less than fifty feet from us, and we would never know it.

Soon after dark, we started to take rocket propelled grenade fire. Most of them ricocheted off of the tank or hit the sand near the tank. It was as dark as night can get. It was almost useless trying to see something in the dense jungle. We had quite a few hits with little effect. One of my crewmen, one of the best with whom I had ever served, got splattered in the face with either sand or shrapnel. It was not serious, but I sent him to the Lieutenant to see what he had to say about it.

The Lieutenant did not seem to care and sent him back. He was walking back, when a trip flair that was set in the barbed wire went off directly in front of my tank. A trip flair is a small device set into the wire or bush. When the wire of the flair was stretched, it let off a burst of bright light, letting you know it had been tripped. I opened up with the sky mounted fifty caliber where I saw the trip flair go off. I got quite a few good bursts out there. My crew man told me later he did not know what to do, hit the dirt, run back to the Lieutenant's tank, or return to his own. He said that he saw the very bright light of the trip flair, and from his position, I was in the middle of it firing the fifty caliber. He said it looked eerie. He chose to come back to my tank. After this incident, the rocket propelled grenades stopped.

This was another operation I did not expect to live through. The grunts were very happy to see us for support, but they seemed very uneasy, even for hardened grunts. They said, "We **will** get overrun tonight. We almost did last night." That made us feel very uneasy.

The Lieutenant decided that at a predetermined time the tanks would open up with all of the guns we had. It was meant to show them what we were capable of. When the time came, each tank opened fire with the thirty caliber machine guns, the fifty caliber machine gun, and the ninety millimeter main gun. It was quite a commotion, and apparently it was heard all the way to Da Nang. We were probably four miles from there.

Soon, the grunt's Commanding Officer back in Da Nang called the grunts' Company Commander in our compound and wanted to know what the hell was going on. When our Lieutenant explained the reason to him, he was infuriated. My Battalion Commander back in Da Nang got into it and told my Lieutenant that if we could not use our tactics the way we wanted to, we were pulling out. My first thought was, "I hope like hell that it is not tonight." I could just imagine it, three tanks, alone at night without lights on, trying to find our way back. It would never work.

Very early in the morning, the grunts sent out a patrol. Right in front of my tank, where the trip flair had gone off, there was a rocket propelled grenade and a gruesome amount of blood that trailed off into the jungle. There was so much blood that there must have been more than one wounded, and it must have been pretty bad for them to have left the RPG behind. I believe that the trip flair saved my life.

This is one time that I did not want to leave the grunts. I felt so sorry for them. I could see the look on their faces as we left. They looked hopeless as we pulled out. Many years later, in Washington DC, I ran into one of the grunts that was there. I asked him what happened, and he said that they were okay. They got reinforced with another company of grunts. When something like that happens, you almost never know the outcome.

We headed back through the leper colony with the lepers staring at us and us at them - the lepers out of despair and us out of morbid curiosity. It was like when you see a car accident. You want to turn away, but you just cannot.

South China Sea

The South China Sea was a beautiful area on the beach. We were stationed in hootches there. It was sandy and tropical with beautiful trees and shrubs. There were very few bugs and nothing like the creepy giant centipedes. It was like a tropical paradise. There was an Am Trk sunk about thirty feet off the shore. It had a large hole in it. There was a large shark that claimed it for his home. He was probably about eight feet from head to tail. We would swim close to him on occasions, and he would swim close to us. The water was a crystal clear blue. I loved it there. It was like a vacation spot.

We were entitled to a week of rest and recuperation every three or four months. We could go to places like Australia, Japan, Hawaii, and Taiwan. I chose not to take R&R. Once I left Vietnam I did not want to come back. One of the guys eventually talked me into going to Yokahama, Japan with him.

We were at the South China Sea Platoon Headquarters, and all was well. Someone brought a puppy into the main hootch where we all hung out. Usually, everyone had to agree before anyone could bring something like that in. Somehow, this pup just appeared. He was a cute little guy, so he was accepted. You could always tell the difference between dogs raised by Americans and dogs raised by the Vietnamese. The American dogs would bark at you, whereas the Vietnamese dogs would slink away. This dog was definitely American. I was playing with him one evening, and he nipped my finger with his sharp little puppy teeth. It bled a little. The Company Corpsman was there and saw it. I did not think any-thing of it.

We were all set for R&R. We went back to Battalion Headquarters in DaNang. About three hours before our plane was scheduled for take off, I received a radio message to call my Com-pany Headquarters. When I did, it was the Company Corpsman. He informed me that the puppy was acting weird and he suspected rabies, so I could not go on R&R. I was extremely disappointed. After my friend had talked me into it, I had my heart set on it, and to now be told I could not go was very upsetting. My buddy was more upset than I was. He did not want to go alone. I could understand. It is more fun to travel with a friend.

Finally after two hours of radio messages, I was told I could go. The Corpsman said that if it was rabies, it would take a long time to actually come out. The Corpsman was calling all over Da Nang for those two hours trying to get someone to give him more information.

My friend and I enjoyed Japan very much. We spent most of our time in Yokohama. As soon as we got there, a hooker came to talk to us. I hooked up with her, and my buddy hooked up with another girl. I went to the zoo with her. Her name was Cookie. She took me to this exclusive hotel on the side of a mountain. The room had these cool wall panels that slid to the side and exposed mirrors. I remember getting quite drunk many times on this vacation.

Yokohama, Japan

When we returned, the puppy was gone. I found out that they had sent the puppy to quarantine. They said it had distemper and not rabies. Several of the guys asked me if I had shot it. I most certainly had not. What happened was not the puppy's fault. In my mind, he was just doing what puppies do.

One of the favorite things for some of the guys to do at the South China Beach was swim underwater to an unsuspecting Marine and bite him on the calf muscle. When I had it done to me the first couple of times it scared the hell out of me. Of course, that did not stop me from doing it to others though.

We had a nice sand field where we played football every day. It had a huge tree root which I removed with a dose of C-4. It was like R&R for us. It was great.

We had our own cook who cooked mostly what we wanted. Once in a while we would have a steak cookout with beer. It was like a family picnic for us. Had there not been a war, the South China Sea would have been a great place to live.

One person in particular that I remember would get care packages, as we called them, from his wife and mother. He never failed to share his wealth with us. They would be filled with all kinds of goodies: cakes, candy, and breads. It was a heavenly smorgasbord to us after months of C rations.

It was here, at the South China Sea, that one of the guys returned from home. He had been on emergency leave (probably a death in the family). Someone came to me and said, "You have to come over here and hear what this Marine has to say." I had no idea what he was talking about. When we got to the hootch most of the platoon had already gathered there. The guys were eager for information about back home. He said, "Tell the Sarge what you saw back in the world (back in the US)."

The other soldier replied, "They hate us over there. They spit at us and call us baby killers." I could not believe what I was hearing! This cannot be so! He continued, "They throw dirty diapers at us."I was in shock! I thought about how we were fighting for them, for our country! We were risking our lives every day, living in sometimes horrendous conditions so they could have their freedom! What the hell was wrong with those people? I said nothing and just walked out to the company perimeter. I sat by myself, contemplating this information for quite some time. It was a great shock for us. I thought we were kind of heroes. Instead, we were viewed as idiots and barbarians.

I had heard later that college kids and some actors were

hoping for the North Vietnamese to kill all of us Americans. They were wishing for our death while we felt that we were protecting them. They were actually supporting the North Vietnamese. This seemed so unpatriotic to me. They did not know me. I was there to help my country.

Tet

Tet is a holiday in Vietnam. It is the most important and popular holiday in Vietnam. Tet is the Vietnamese New Year, marking the arrival of spring based on the Lunar calendar. The name Tet Nguyên Đán means Feast of the First Morning. It takes place from the first day of the first month of the Lunar calendar (around late January or early February) until at least the third day. In Tet of 1968, there was supposed to be a truce and cease fire, out of respect for the holiday, so the attack of '68 took everyone by surprise. I came to Vietnam near the middle of the '68 Tet. According to the military records, 1968 and 1969 were the years of the heaviest fighting in Vietnam.

I read that Tet of '68 was a devastating defeat for North Vietnam, but our good old news media turned it all around and made it sound like a great victory for North Vietnam. They lost one third of their people and equipment in one large countrywide battle. Did the papers mention that the North Vietnamese were the ones to break the truce and dishonor the holiday?

The North Vietnamese had squads that went around to people who were friendly with the South Vietnamese or United States and executed them. They took whatever they wanted from the people.

Tet of '69 was another time of a countrywide attack. I was on a hill just outside of Da Nang again. We were not hit at all but watched many fire fights out in the jungles. Sometimes I felt sorry for the American Troops that were getting hit, as the fighting looked very furious, and there I was doing nothing.

The next day we traveled some of the countryside on patrols and saw the destruction to the civilian population. I saw a cow on one side of the street that looked like it was sat down by a group of people. Its head was cut off and was sitting in front of a hootch across the street. It was eerie the way it sat there like it was resting. I guess that was a message. I did not understand what it meant, but I am sure the Vietnamese people did.

Some of the US troops hated the Vietnamese people. I felt sorry for them. They were fighting for their homeland. Some of them saw us as foreign invaders. Some of them paid a horrendous price for working with the United States because they felt it was the honorable thing to do.

Almost all of the Vietnam Veterans that I have talked to felt that we could have won that war anytime we wanted to. Most of us felt that the American politicians did not want us to win. The United States, despite what the news media said, never lost a major battle over there. There were so many things that the United States could have done if they really wanted to win. We would take a position at the cost of many lives, pull out a week later, then a month later retake the same old position. Maybe there was a strategy behind it, but I never understood it.

Fifty Caliber

Each platoon had different markings on their tank and different locations of the fifty caliber machine gun. When I first got to Charlie Company, I was put in first platoon where the fifties were copula mounted. I was later transferred to third platoon where the fifties were sky mounted (mounted on top).

My favorite location was on top of the sky mount. It meant you had to have your hatch opened. You were very exposed while firing the machine gun, but you could see very well.

Once, while the fifty caliber was copula mounted, it misfired while we were in a combat situation near C Company Headquarters. I used the manual cocking lever and tried to chamber a new round. It did not work. I opened up the feed cover plate to see if I could figure out the reason that it misfired. Seeing nothing and in my excitement, I used the manual cocking lever to pull the bolt back. I let it fly shut, which was a big mistake with the feed cover plate opened. It must have picked up a round on its way back. The round jammed inside of the machine gun. The extractor lever, which pulls the shot round from the chamber, hit the primer on the round and it fired inside the gun. I had my face very close to see what was going on with the gun.

There was a loud explosion and I felt the powder burn my face. I could not believe what happened! A fifty caliber round fired inches from my face? I did not have much time to think about it, closed the back plate, and chambered another round. Luckily it fired and I resumed shooting.

Thinking about it later, I thanked God again. There were so many things that could have happened. The powder could have burned my eyes. The brass from the round could have injured me. I found the brass from the round later and was surprised that it was shredded on the end. I never found the bullet itself. I still have that brass somewhere in my home. I never saw that happen before or after that single incident.

The fifty caliber was developed as an anti-aircraft weapon but was quickly put to use against troops and unarmored vehicles. It had a very long range and packed one hell of a punch. The effective range is approximately two thousand yards, and they could stray to about seven thousand yards.

The marking on the tanks were whatever every one agreed on. Sometimes we had Playboy bunnies and sometimes a Maltese cross.

The first tank in the platoon had one bunny on the barrel of the ninety millimeter main gun. The second tank had two bunnies and so on up to the final and fifth tank. One of the guys who was somewhat of an artist did the painting. They were also painted on the search light cover. Each tank had a search light tank which had an extremely bright light above the main gun.

Example of Tank Markings
Courtesy of David Forsyth

The Guys

Jerry Holly was the driver on the tanks I commanded for quite some time. He liked being a driver and stayed at that position. He was a true Marine. He did what he was told. He would tell you if he did not like it, but he would still do it. I tried to promote him to gunner several times, but he did not like that position, so I let him stay as the driver. He had certain guidelines he expected everyone to follow. If you followed them, he was your best friend. If not, he did not have much use for you. He felt everyone should respect their seniors. I liked Jerry and had a great amount of respect for him.

Jerry Holly

I was down to about a month to go before I rotated out of the Nam. Someone asked if I would like to ride to Battalion Headquarters. I said that I would go. It would be nice to see some of the guys in the rear. They told us to pick up a new guy who was going to our platoon. As was the custom, we seldom introduced ourselves. We just said, "Jump in". No one wore rank insignias in the field. It would have been like wearing a red light - SHOOT ME FIRST! As we were driving back, we started to talk. He said, not knowing who I was, that the guys in battalion headquarter told him to try to get on Sergeant Hoch's tank. "He is the best." I was very flattered and I did put him on my tank. His name, I later found out, was Todd Phillips.

Jerry and Todd stayed in contact for all those years after Vietnam. Jerry kept trying to find out where I was, but he couldn't recall my first name (he was pretty sure it wasn't really Sarge). Gary Mefford, the Communications Sergeant, found Jerry through the Vietnam Tanker's Association. Either Gary told him my first name or he figured it out on his own, because after thirty years, he finally located me. Gary was the one who called me. We had a reunion in Las Vegas. It was with the last tank crew I had in Vietnam, along with Gary. We had an old black and white photo of us in front of our tank in Vietnam. We did the same pose in Las Vegas. There was probably a two hundred pounds difference from the Nam photo to the Las Vegas photo.

Soon after I rotated out of the Nam, Jerry and my old tank crew, with a new Tank Commander, were sent on a stupid mission dreamed up by someone who wanted to be a hero.

His tank (which was my old tank with a new Commander) was struck by an RPG. Portions of it hit a box of fifty caliber ammo sitting on the fender near the driver's hatch. Parts of the RPG hit Jerry in the neck, severely wounding him.

He received a Bronze Star and a Purple Heart for this operation. Soon after he left the Marine Corps, he worked for an auto manufacturing company. He later became a police officer for the Great Lakes Naval Yard. It was there that he was awarded two medals for bravery. One was for grabbing someone who was going to jump off of a building, I think. One was for going into a burning building to save two children.

I saw Jerry in Las Vegas along with the rest of my last tank crew and the Communications Sergeant. It was the first time we were together in thirty years. It was a great feeling to be with them after all those years. I felt so safe and comfortable with them. It was like the old days when we watched out for each other. Some bonds just do not fade over time.

Jerry told me that he felt I was a role model for him, and he tried to follow my example throughout his life. I do not think I ever received a better compliment, especially from someone I respected as much as I respected him.

In Las Vegas he weighed approximately two hundred and forty muscular pounds. I saw him last in Washington D.C. where he weighed one hundred and twenty seven pounds. He had terminal cancer. He asked me to be one of his pall bearers at his funeral. I was honored to do so. The last thing I said to him, with tears in my eyes, was, "Jerry, what can I say." He said, "Nothing, absolutely nothing."

I flew to Kenosha, Wisconsin to be his pall bearer. He died on November tenth, the Marine Corps' birthday. What a fitting day for him to go. I believe he planned it that way.

I also had the privilege of meeting his wonderful wife and two wonderful children, who respected him very much also. Jerry was a Sergeant in the police force and retired a Lieutenant. It amazed me that after all those years he still called me Sarge.

Jerry once said to me, "I wish you were there when I got wounded."

I said, "I am very glad I wasn't."

He said, "It would have been a totally different outcome had you been there."

Todd and I are still good friends. He now lives in Vermont, and we communicate often through e-mail or on the phone. Jerry always credited Todd with saving his life when he was seriously wounded after I went home. I am grateful that he did.

Gary received the Navy Achievement Medal for Leadership and was promoted to Staff Sergeant. He went back to college after his service time and became a teacher. He later became a principal and retired as one. He now has his own construction business. I always knew he would be successful!

Ski was different. He usually didn't hang with the rest of us. He seemed to always have some ailment. He had an opinion on everything. But despite all of that, he was a genuinely good person. He always wore his cover (hat) far back on his head.

I remember once when he was driving a tank that I was commanding. We were going through thick bush country. He

Jerry, Todd, Ski, Clyde, Gary
Our First Meeting in Vegas

Vietnam 1969
Top Row: Clyde Hoch, Richard Gerszewski (Ski)
Bottom Row: Jerry Holly, Todd Phillips

Las Vegas 2004
Top Row: Clyde Hoch, Richard Gerszewski (Ski)
Bottom Row: Jerry Holly, Todd Phillips

slammed the brake on the tank so suddenly that it rocked back and forth. He stopped so quickly that it surprised us all. I said over the intercom, "Ski, what happened?" I thought he may have seen a large bomb that was a dud or some other ordinance that didn't go off.

He replied, "A rat!!"

I said, "A rat?!?! You stopped for a damned rat?!?"

He said "Yeah! Look at it!" I walked out on the fender and knelt next to him. He pointed at the area where he saw the alleged rodent. I saw a large lizard. We all took out our 45 pistols and fired at it. No one hit it as it scampered away.

I said to him, "Ski, where the hell are you from?"

He said, "New York."

I said, "Well that explains that."

Ski and I were together for quite some time in Vietnam. It seemed that most places I went, he was there also. I didn't mind, though. He was a good Marine and always did what was asked of him.

I knew he had health issues later on. When we met in Vegas, Todd had to catch him as he passed out in a chair at breakfast. When he passed away, no one knew about it until someone saw his obituary. We all felt bad that we could not be there at his bedside and attend his funeral.

Welcome Home!

It was near the end of my Vietnam tour when our Platoon Sergeant was promoted to Platoon Commander. He told me I was now the Platoon Sergeant, usually a position held by someone with much more time in the Marines than I had. He also informed me that I was selected for Staff Sergeant. The Commandant of the Marine Corps signs a Staff Sergeant warrant. He only signs so many a month and each had a number assigned. It was after I got out of the service that my warrant finally caught up to me. By now they had changed the title to Staff Sergeant in the Reserves. I also received a Navy/Marine Achievement Medal with the Combat V for outstanding leadership at that time.

My time was running short. I went on my last operation just days before I was to go home. It was my choice to do so. I had it in my mind that I would never leave Vietnam alive. I felt that if nothing else happened, the plane would get shot down on the way home.

I went to countless briefings for countless operations. The guys would always ask me, "What's going to happen?"

I would say, "This one is no sweat." I thought to myself so many times, "Tomorrow is going to be pure Hell." I always kept that part to myself.

There were so many times I went to sleep thinking that I would not last to see the morning sun come up. There were so many days I woke up and said to myself, "This one will surely be my last day on earth." Some how I made it through them all. So did most of the guys. I am sure all of the ones who made it had similar feelings.

There were so many close calls that I don't remember them all. Some one once told me, "You came back because God has a purpose for you!" Now I am sure he was right.

I could not believe it! I was on my way home. I had seen my share of combat and survived. Little did I know, my biggest battles were yet to come.

When I left Vietnam, I would have three months to serve in the states. After being on my own so much in Vietnam, I did not look forward to the disciplinary regime in the States. I received orders for Drill Instructor School. I asked to stay in Vietnam to finish out my time. They said no! They needed drill instructors too badly. To some Marines, getting drill instructor duty was the ultimate. To me you kind of had to be a dick to be a drill instructor. I did not want to treat people that way so I chose to get out. I got out three months early with thirty days leave time, so it was really two months early.

After discharge my parents picked me up at a train station. The greeting was, "Hi! How are you! Good to see you again!" It was a quiet ride. I thought about what kind of a job I could get. What could I do? I wished I had a girlfriend. It would have been more comforting than being greeted by my estranged parents. When we did get home, there was no neighborhood greeting! There was barely a greeting at all. I was shocked to see that the dog I had for so many years was in terrible shape. I soon took him to the Vet to put him to sleep. I had brought the dog home as a young boy. We were always together if I was not in school. It was just the start of the pain and loneliness that I would feel being back home.

Now I felt so much more alone. I left Vietnam feeling important and useful to society, even though I felt as though society did not like me. Society hated us because we were trained killers in their eyes. Now I had no real friends, no job. I had no girlfriend. When I left, everyone else had gone on with their lives. I felt useless. I had no one to talk to about it. I started to hang out in bars way too much. I couldn't even talk about Vietnam in bars. It always led to an argument or a fight. There was always a stupid comment, "What is it like to kill women and children?" There was a never ending supply of stupid comments. The really short hair during that time period was a dead give away that you were military.

I lived at home with my parents. Before I had left for Vietnam, one of my brothers-in-law gave me a lot of German military medals and badges that he had picked up in WWII. I treasured them. I often wondered why he had not given them to his own children. Maybe he knew that I would treasure them and take care of them. My mother let one of my nephews stay in my room while

I was gone. When I returned home all of these items were gone, along with a very nice throwing knife that I had bought when I was in Germany. I was pissed. How rude and disrespectful. Talk about depression setting in.

I finally found a job, which I did not like very much. I was working in a place where I was a grinder, cleaning up welds. The people that worked with me were much older than I was, and they really gave me a hard time. One comment will always stick in my mind. I bought a coffee and dumped a slight portion of it out so I could pour some water into it to cool it off. One of the guys said, "You must be rich as hell to afford to throw coffee away." Of course, I was not, he knew it, and I resented the comment. They gave me a hard time every chance they got. I hated it. To make matters worse it was the night shift. Humans are not nocturnal. We were not meant to be up all night and sleep during the day. It made me cranky.

I remember one time a supervisor gave me a job to do. I was young and ambitious, and I wanted to succeed. I finished the job and went back to him. I said, "I'm finished with that job. What do you want me to do next?"

He actually got angry and said, "Well then do this. It should take you the rest of the night." He gave me another chore which he wanted me to make last until the end of the shift. I was puzzled. Here was a supervisor who got angry with me for trying to do my best! Everywhere I went, I tried hard and was condemned for it. So I tried to slow down. I tried hard to slow down and failed at this also. I was always in a hurry and never really going anywhere.

I took to hunting again because I liked the solitude. My big brother had started me hunting. When I was younger he used to take me with him. When I got home from Vietnam, I just didn't even think about it anymore. I made a new acquaintance, and he asked me to go hunting with him. "Just go out once", he said. I got back into it. I liked to walk the woods on a nice crisp cold morning. It was quiet. I would run into a deer every once in a while. Most of the time I would enjoy just watching it as it tossed its head looking for me. I loved the challenge of sneaking up on deer.

At this point in my life I became less social and more

withdrawn. I hated being in crowds. I hated to go to clubs where there were a lot of people. I became very tense during these times. Weddings and birthday parties were very difficult for me to bare. I had a hard time hearing, especially with a lot of back ground noise like lots of people talking at once or loud music. I could hear them but could not understand them. I did not want to sound stupid by continuously asking people what they said so I would just say yes and not really understand the conversation. I avoided these situations at all cost. I really did not like my life or myself. I became a real loner. I did not fit in anywhere in the States.

Soon one of my old friends started to come around. I began hanging out with him. He was also a Marine and had served in Vietnam. It was comforting because we could talk about it together. He and I went to his friend's house and hung out there. Soon an old girlfriend started to show up. She had just left her husband, and she had taken her two children she had with him. One thing led to another, and some time later she moved in with me. I eventually married her. The father of the children died. I felt so sorry for them. Every child should have a father so I adopted them. We had two more children together. Then it all fell apart, and we separated. I was devastated for the loss of the children. I missed them so much. I still saw the children every other weekend, all four of them.

Once again I was coming home to an empty house and started to hang out in bars. I met a young woman. We seemed to get along well. Sometime later, she moved in. Everything went well for a time and then, probably mostly my fault, she moved out. She was a nice, quiet girl who held everything in until she would just burst with anger and lash out terribly. I hated these outbursts, but I should have been more understanding.

Back to the bars, again. Soon after I met another woman, and we started dating. She seemed to get along well with my children. We married and had a child together. She was hard to live with, but she would probably say the same about me. We had a very rocky road, but she stayed with me. Why she did, I will never know. It was only through her insistence that we did stay together. We are very different people. I was very unhappy with my job and my life, but she hung in there. Now we are at the point where we are comfortable with each other.

I never had a job I really liked. I assumed my life was no different than anyone else's, though. I had a job I did not like. I had a wife I did not get along with. It seems to be pretty typical in this country.

To this day, I have a hard time hearing in crowds and I tend to avoid them. I have a job that I am not really passionate about, although I continually do the best I can do. I have been working hard to adjust my life where I can so I can get along with most people. I regret every day that I did not live my life differently. I wish I had a career that I enjoyed. I wish I would have worked less and tried to have a much better quality of life. I have done things to people I deeply regret. I have broken every one of the Ten Commandments at one time or another. I now feel that I have a lot of making up to do with God, so I do whatever I can for other people.

I was told once that I was a good father to the children. I have never felt like I was. I feel I was more concerned for my needs than theirs. I wish I would have been much better to them. They all became fine adults, in spite of everything. I never talked to them or anyone else about Vietnam because I did not think that anyone would care what I had to say. Someone once said to me, "You never told me you are a war hero."

I replied, "That is because I am not. I was just an ordinary person doing what I was trained to do. I am not a hero, and I never will be."

I think the hardest thing I had to get used to back in the states was the lack of respect people had for each other. In the Marine Corps we respected each other and totally relied on each other. We were taught respect.

Retrospect

I did not write this book earlier in my life because no one wanted to hear about Vietnam. I write this now from memory, in the hopes that someone reads it, gains knowledge, and maybe some understanding, from it.

After coming home from Vietnam we seldom mentioned being there at all because it usually broke into an argument or a fist fight. As everyone knows, we Vietnam Vets were considered the scum of the earth by most civilians in the United States. I have heard lots of comments, "You guys lost that war", "Vietnam was a conflict, it wasn't even a war", and "You cannot join the VFW, because it wasn't a real war". Obviously the people who called it a conflict weren't there. I still think that 95% of the population have no idea what happened in Vietnam. Maybe they just do not care. After seeing a drunk passed out, one of my friends (who was not a vet) said to a group of us that he must be a Vietnam Vet. The American media made it seem like the Vietnam vets were all drug addicts and alcoholics. From what I saw, quite the opposite was true.

If you try to find the negative in something, eventually you will. The American public and media were looking for reasons to hate the Vietnam Vets. Trust me, the feeling is mutual. I lost contact with everyone I was with in Vietnam, or Nam as we called it, for about thirty years. Nobody wanted to associate with us, so we just did not talk about it. It was in the past, and we went on with our lives. We just tucked that portion of our lives into a small box in our hearts and minds.

It was horrible to see a fellow Marine with severe wounds getting helped by a Corpsman. I was never good at this and had to give the Corpsman great credit. I could not do his job. It was much more horrible to see a young child, dead from wounds, being held by his crying and moaning mother. I saw both many times. It never got easier.

I have always felt that the Vietnamese people were merely pawns of the war. I now feel that we were all pawns - the South Vietnamese, the North, the Australians, the Koreans, the Navy,

Army, Air Force, and Marines. I felt then, as I do now, that we could have won that war anytime that we wanted to. It was started and kept going, in my opinion, by big business. War is good for the economy, which is really good for the large business owners and the politicians. Our politicians helped to get us there and kept us there because they had their hands in the pockets of the big corporations. For this reason, I feel our politics and big business are in a horrible mess. I do not understand how they could send people to war for their own profits.

I do not feel too much sympathy for people who came home and readjusted (not without difficulty) to civilian life, like I did. I feel so sorry for people who are yet in Veteran's hospitals for various reasons, and no one cares at all about them. We reach out to help other countries in need, but our own veterans are purposely put away and forgotten about because they are a blemish on the face of the United States of America.

The Marines in Vietnam were some of the best people I have ever met in my life. We were a very close-knit group. I only recall one fight among Americans. I do not recall what it was about, but you have to remember that we were in a very tense situation, too. We needed each other. You looked out for the other guy because he looked out for you. He had your back. Never in my life did I ever feel so protected by the people around me. Ironic, isn't it? It was extremely hard for me to get used to coming back to the states where there was so much backstabbing, selfishness, and arrogance. I almost felt like going back to Vietnam.

We as a society are passing down the wrong road. We admire and respect the wrong ambitions and professions. We idolize actors, athletes, and CEO's who are not in tune with the life of everyday people, instead of the person in the military who has risked their life and given so much of themselves.

I was a Sergeant in the Marine Corps. I had a lot of power. I was in charge of two or three tanks, sometimes five tanks, plus the men that crewed them. I was responsible for them and their well being seven days a week for twenty four hours a day in combat. My superiors usually left me alone to promote or demote whom I chose. The men came to me with almost all their problems, and

I felt it was my job to help them as best as I could. At times, my superiors came to me with problems.

Sometimes with that power came an inflated ego. Most times it was very heavy like a yoke around my neck. I constantly worried that I would screw up and get some of our guys killed. This was always heavy on my mind and on my heart. These men had families that were counting on them to come home, and I felt responsible for making sure that they made it there.

When I returned to civilian life, I was just one of many punk kids who just got out of the military. I received no respect and worked very hard to fit back into civilian life.

I was told once, "You lost that war. It was the only one the US has ever lost." The men and women who served in Vietnam never lost a major battle. In WWII many riflemen never fired a shot in combat. I am not sure why, maybe out of fear. Our military realized this and made up a new training program, which changed it to almost one hundred percent of the troops firing their weapons in Vietnam. In my mind, our politicians and the American public lost that war.

The people I served with are the finest people I have ever met. They were truly honorable in combat, and I am very proud to have served with them. Whenever I hear a negative comment about Vietnam Veterans, it infuriates me. Not so much for me but for the finest people America has to offer.

Through the US Marine Corps Vietnam Tankers Association, I began to receive phone calls from the guys I served with in Vietnam. Al, from the Med cruise, called me at two o'clock in the morning years ago. He filled me in on his life. I asked for his address, but he said he would not be there long. I did not hear from him for another fifteen years. My youngest daughter had just finished a course on Vietnam in college when Al called me again. About a week later, many of the guys started calling me. I felt that the timing was pretty ironic. We all decided to meet in Las Vegas in 2004 with our wives. My whole last tank crew and the Communications Sergeant were there. We had a great time catching up and talking about the past. The one hotel we went to was in the old part of town. There was a screen over the street, really high up. At night they would do LED light displays on it. We would sit around drinking and watching it.

After that first get-together, we started meeting in Washington DC for the Marine Corps Birthday on November 10th and Veteran's Day on November 11th. There were about six or seven of us that would go every year. Since then, three of them have died. Two of them died from prostate cancer, which has been linked to Agent Orange.

When I was in Vietnam, for about two hundred feet around every compound we were in, there was no vegetation of any kind. I asked one of the officers about it once. He said that it was sand and nothing grew in sand. Even at the time, I knew he was full of shit, because there was vegetation beyond that in the sand. I never even heard of Agent Orange until ten years after I was out of the service. I read as much as I could find on it and found out it was basically a herbicide defoliant that killed all of the vegetation it touched or contacted. I wonder if it was FDA approved, not that it would matter. I was told later that it was most heavily used in the area that I was in, and also during the same time period of my service in Vietnam. I read an article that the Vietnam Vets are dying at a rate of four hundred ninety nine people per day.

It seems like now it is popular to be a Vietnam Vet, and millions of people claim to be Vietnam Vets. I work with a guy who claimed to be a Vietnam Vet. When I questioned him about it, he said that he was in the service during that time. Even though he never went to Vietnam, he considered himself a Vietnam Vet. Those people are called Vietnam Era Veterans.

I feel that most people have a great distrust of me. I think a lot of that comes from the fact that I look like a very serious person. On the inside I am not, but that is how I think I am perceived. I wanted and tried very hard for people to like me, but I feel I failed miserably. I do not really have any close friends. Now I wonder if it is because I really do not like myself.

In Vietnam, I was doing the most patriotic, noble thing. I was fighting for my country. In the Marines, I was rewarded for doing my job well. I could think on my feet. I protected and saved many people, and I was well respected. Coming home was a culture shock to me. This country does not do a very good job of reintegrating soldiers back into society. At least they did not back then. I had such conflicting messages. I was hated. I did my time in the military, but there was nothing left for me afterward. How could I like myself when the country hated me? I risked my life for our government, only to come home and be treated like dirt. I was not allowed to talk about Vietnam, but in some ways, it was the high point of my life. In other ways, it was a nightmare that I cannot forget to this day. Some people had it far worse than I did, and some had it much better.

I do not think I ever really dealt with my feelings about Vietnam, which is why I keep to myself. Maybe that is why I decided to write my memoirs. Not many people go through what I have gone through and live to tell about it. I cannot imagine any of them **not** having emotional and psychological issues to work through. I have learned that everyone has a different perspective on life. This is mine. I hope your perspective changes as you learn and grow. I hope you have compassion for others, whether you agree with how they lived their lives or not.

Stories From Fellow Vietnam Veterans

Phantom Painter
by Jim Littman

Charlie Company had a phantom painter who would, every chance he got, paint something in the camp. The Commanding Officer took the prank in stride. He warned us all if any of us got caught with painting part of the company area, we would have trouble on their hands. Well, one night the phantom painter struck again, painting the head (bathroom) inside and outside. It was late at night. The CO had finished playing cards with a group of men in his tent and went to use the head. When he returned and went to climb into bed, everyone in the tent began to laugh. The CO was not amused by the target on his back side. We all stood tall that night with the threat of the club being closed; and until the phantom painter fessed up there would be a lot of extra duty available. The phantom painter fessed up, but I still think the CO checked the seat whenever he sat down.

Welcome to Charlie Company
by Gary Mefford

There was a very interesting welcoming tradition in Vietnam. I am not absolutely sure if it was the welcoming tradition
when I first hit battalion (December '67) or if it was when I got
to Charlie Company (shortly after TET in '68). I have a feeling it
was when I first hit Viet Nam and was stationed at Bn for a couple
of months before being transferred to Charlie Company to assume
the duties of Company Communications Chief.

I reported to my new duty station and had a relatively nice
looking uniform with new-looking jungle utilities, jungle boots
(with webbing on the sides so your feet could breathe), and a cover
(hat). Maybe the purpose of this exercise was to make the new guy
not stand out so much from the others who had been "in country"
for awhile and whose uniforms were soiled, torn, and pretty shabby
looking.

Once I checked in and settled in, I was greeted by many
Marines who came to welcome me. I believe they were mostly
tankers, but some might have been in communications. They
were very happy to welcome me to the unit and told me they had
a welcoming ritual. At first I was uneasy and wondered just what
this ritual might entail. I had heard stories about college and frat
pledges going through some unusual initiation and hazing activi-
ties. They reassured me that I would enjoy the experience.

They took me to a rather remote area in the tank lot where
tanks and tank parts were staged. In the sand there was a large
round steel hub looking chunk of metal that looked like a rounded
cap. I later found out it was a hatch for a tank. It was marked like
a sliced pie with values on each slice. I was told I would be given
a sledge hammer and would be positioned close to the "target"
and I would move around in a circle and continue to hit the target
with the sledge hammer as many times as I could and as often as
I could. "Okay", I thought, "I can do that. Sounds pretty easy."
They positioned me and prepared me for the event. Then, they
asked if I was ready and I confirmed I was.

"Oh," one of them said, "we forgot to tell you that you do

this blindfolded."

"Oh yeah," I thought.

So, someone got a cloth to use as the blindfold and another Marine said, "Hey, let me take your cover." My cover was removed and the blindfold was in place. They asked if I could see anything. I could not. They repositioned me and had me circle the metal one time and asked if I was ready. I was. They said to hold the sledge hammer out at arm's length so I would be the right distance away from the target. I was told the harder I hit the target, the more points I would earn. Then, they went into the "Ready, set, go" command. I began. Each time I hit the target harder, I was cheered on with shouts, hoorahs, applause, and other encouraging cheers to continue earning points. The more cheers I got, the harder I hit the target and the faster I went around the circle. I was digging a ring in the sand as I shuffled around the target. I remember taking the sledge hammer as far to the rear as I could and swinging as hard as I could. It didn't take too much of this activity to wear me out. I don't know how many times I hit that heavy metal chuck, but I did a pretty good job. When I stopped, more cheering and applause came and they asked if I was done. I said that I was. They took my blindfold off and everyone started to laugh, cheer, and applaud. There, on top of the "target" was my cover. They had placed it there and had continually moved it to the top of the striking surface while I wound up for another swing. I had pretty much demolished my cover. It was ceremoniously placed on my head and someone said a few words and told me that I was to wear this tattered, frayed, ripped, and beaten to hell cover with pride while in this unit, so I did.

Gary Qualifying With His Hat

M67 Flame Tank Firing

The Big Viet Cong
By Gary Mefford

I have had to get some assistance from my friend Doc
Forsyth on particular instances. It was February 22, 1969 and all
seemed normal and usual, until shortly after midnight. At two thirty in the morning, all Hell broke loose. We got hit with mortars,
gas, and got infiltrated through a bunker. The Marines who were on
watch had been smoking pot and were impervious as to what was
going on.

We were abruptly awakened by incoming and everyone
started to scramble to get to wherever they needed to be during an
attack. I was the Communications Chief of the company and my
responsibility was the company communications bunker. That was
where I had communications staff assigned around the clock so
we would have contact with our battalion, our four platoons (headquarters, first, second, and third) that would usually be assigned to
support outlying infantry units (local infantry battalions and companies), and support units such as artillery, MedEvac, etc.

I was sleeping in my NCO (Non Commissioned Officer)
hootch when this barrage began early that morning. When I was
awakened, I instinctively started for the communications bunker
(aka comm bunker). I ran outside and it was pitch dark. We had
mortars dropping everywhere and everyone was scrambling to get
to their assigned stations. There were Viet Cong infiltrators running
and screaming. Marines were just shooting towards the screaming
and running. The VC were actually drawing fire from all the Marines, and we were shooting at one another from all sides. It was
utter chaos. The VC were not concerned about their lives. Their
only concern was to kill or help kill as many Americans as they
could. It was just another guerrilla warfare tactic that was used
during the war. On my way to the comm bunker, I ran through a
curtain of stench. We had been hit by tear gas! My thoughts were
to get to the comm bunker, but I had already started with the water-
ing eyes and running nose. I decided that I needed to go back to
my hootch and get my gas mask. So, I turned around and headed
back to my hootch. I ran into the hootch, even though it was pitch

dark, to get my gas mask and relief from the tear gas.

There were momentary flashes of light as illumination rounds went off between the mortar shells. As I ran into the hootch, I was hit in the forehead and knocked down on my back. Who was that, and how could he knock me down? I got up and bolted forward again – only to knocked to my ass again. How could a Viet Cong be big enough to knock me to the ground? Now my entire face was covered with the water from my eyes and my running nose. The stench was burning my skin, and I was miserable. But I had to get past the huge VC that was keeping me from getting to my area and gas mask. I gathered all my strength to get through the SOB this time. Again I got knocked down! I was hard pressed. How he could see me in the dark? Why did he continue to strike me down and not shoot me?

As I laid on my back, another illumination round went off, and I saw for the first time what was not letting me get to my gas mask. Our hootch was a tent with lumber reinforcing the walls, ceilings, and rafters. A mortar had hit our hootch after I had exited to get to the comm bunker and the mortar had broken some of the ceiling joists, which had fallen down into the hootch. Each time I ran to my area, I hit the ceiling joist dead on in the middle of my forehead. After crawling under the broken two by eight, I got my gas mask on, cleared it, and made it to the comm bunker. I had three big goose eggs to prove the injury for days afterward. However, I do not think I ever admitted how I got the injury to anyone other than Fred Hoekstra and Doc Forsyth as I was pretty embarrassed to be struck down that night by a two by eight!

The Enlisted Men's Club After An Attack
Courtesy of Gary Mefford

Changing Times
by Private Todd Phillips

You know, I have had people ask me how the war changed me. I know it did to some extent. You cannot go through what we did, see and do some of the things that we did (at the tender age of eighteen, no less) without some effect. But I think what really changed me was coming home. When we were in the Corp and Nam, we always had each other. There was always a brotherhood and a code we lived by. When I got home, everything from the music to the clothes had changed. When I left, I had never heard of drugs, or hippies, or protesters. I was from a small town. We didn't even have a race problem. But I guess everything changed after they killed John, Bobby, and Martin.

Not everyone had a problem with us. Many of the old people and most of the WW2 vets treated us pretty well sometimes. When the WW2 vets came home, everyone was glad to see them. Their war was over. When we came home, our war was still going on. You couldn't get away from it. They were burning draft cards and flags. I must admit, I kind of liked it when the girls burned their bras. They were marching on D.C. and Haute Ashberry was going on. The flower child. For a generation that preached peace and love, I sure felt hated and alone.

I wonder why it is so popular to be a Vietnam Vet now, when we were looked down on for so long! Hell, you even have people lying about being there!

Doc Comes Home
by David (Doc) Forsyth

"How many did you kill, you son of a bitch!" The words were screamed from somewhere behind me, and they seemed somehow out of context on a domestic commercial airplane.

I was returning to "CONUS," on my way "Back to the World." I was on my way home. My tour in Vietnam was over and I had survived. I wanted to leave, it was time. Two years earlier I had requested, seven times in all, to be trained as an FMF Corpsman and to be attached to a Marine combat unit. My wishes, after such persistence, had been granted. And now the experience was behind me or rather seared into me. My psyche had been forever altered, and my view of the world permanently skewed. But tonight I was heading east from Los Angeles, headed back to Florida, to my parents, my family, my home.

My tour in Nam, by comparison and in retrospect, had gone well. Anyone who experiences a year of combat duty and is upright and ambulatory at the end of it can easily say it went well. I had twenty or so days left on my tour when a request had been made by the Red Cross that I return home. My father, a retired Marine Lt Col., was very ill and about to undergo two surgeries simultaneously. I was ordered to pack my gear, head to Da Nang and then back to Florida to be with him.

When the plane lifted from the tarmac, I wept, for what I wasn't sure as there were just too many emotions to deal with - a flood of overwhelming, indecipherable emotions that left me both elated and dazed. I was overjoyed to have survived and elated to be leaving but at the same time extraordinarily sad. I felt horribly guilty to be leaving, and as odd as it may seem . . . to be alive.

This leg of the flight was to Okinawa. I was then to continue aboard a MATS flight scheduled to leave sometime in the afternoon the following day. I was able to secure a bunk in a transient barracks and took a long hot shower which felt great, even though I had no clean uniform to change into afterwards. I was still wearing my filthy jungle utilities, but what the hell, I was beginning to feel human again.

The next day I was summoned to the airfield and told there was a possibility that I could board a civilian chartered flight for my return. I was hustled aboard and seated when a couple of ambulatory wounded Marines were boarded. After checking the manifest, they were told there was a mistake and they were about to be hustled off because there were not enough seats. I told one of them to take my seat, I'd catch another flight and then someone else followed suit and offered his seat to the other wounded Marine. I could wait. Besides, these were my Marines, and I would for the rest of my days feel an obligation to and responsibility for every one of them.

The MATS flight was set for the next morning and rather than go back to the barracks I chose to hunker down in a corner of the terminal and wait. The next day came rather quickly as I recall, and I was shuffled aboard a C-130 transport bound for somewhere in South Carolina. There were about eight or ten of us, cradled in cargo netting in the bay. A member of the flight crew gave us a brief safety talk, and we started down the runway, finally heading home. But less than five minutes into the flight, that same crew member descended the ladder from the cockpit and informed us that there was a problem with the landing gear. We would be returning to Okinawa. What a disappointment.

We returned to the airfield and deplaned. Another six or eight hours had lapsed when we were once again ordered to board our "Freedom Bird." While still on the ascent from our take off, the cockpit door slammed open and a crewman jumped into the cargo hold, screaming at us to extinguish all cigarettes, there was a fuel leak and possibly a fire aboard! "Be prepared to ditch!" Jeeze! Was I ever going to get off this island?

The plane made it back in one piece. We were once again evacuated from the aircraft and told to stand-bye for further orders. I found a spot and hunkered down in the terminal once again and waited. The next day I was told there was an opening on another civilian chartered flight if I wanted it. I did. I'd been told that the third time is a charm, and in this case it turned out to be true . . . sort of. After a fuel stop in Guam, or maybe it was Wake island, we finally landed at Travis AFB in California. I shared a cab with someone to LA where I bought a ticket to Florida via Houston Texas. The crew aboard the National Airlines plane were great and despite my smelly mud and blood stained jungle utilities, they offered me a seat in First class and handed me a scotch. I was grateful and very pleased to be on American soil, headed home.

The plane was scheduled to make a short stop in Houston before continuing on to Miami. As we descended into Houston the flight attendant made her announcements and prepared the cabin for landing. We were on final approach when I heard it . . . from somewhere behind me. "How many did you kill, you son of a bitch?" I wondered what the commotion was. I turned in my seat to look back, and it was then that I heard the footsteps, heavy, and coming fast. I never saw him really. He was on me before I knew it. He grabbed me around the neck and started throwing punches and screaming. I immediately grabbed for my seat belt, released it, got up, punched him three or four times and took him to the deck.

The passengers began screaming as I wrestled the man to the floor. As I recall, the plane was just touching down when the first officer burst out of the cockpit and ran toward me. It was at that moment that my attackers buddy jumped on my back. Now I was fighting two of them, and with all due respect, it was not a fair fight... for them. The National Airlines first officer grabbed the guy on my back and pushed him off of me. I then picked up the guy I'd first been fighting with and slammed him into the bulkhead and shoved my boot into his neck. For the moment everything seemed to be under control.

It was what came next that has haunted me most about this incident. The passengers who had witnessed this brawl, up close and personal, began screaming at me, pleading with me not to kill him. "Don't kill him! Please, don't!" I was astonished. I was flattened by their words. Kill him? Who did they think I was? He may have been drunk, he may have been mentally deranged, or he may have just been an asshole, but I wasn't going to kill him! My God, I thought, what do they think of us? What do they think we've become? I am a Nam Vet. I am also your son, your brother, father, neighbor... a fellow American. Or am I?

When the cabin door was opened FBI and FAA officials

boarded the plane and dragged the two offenders off into the darkness. I was asked to deplane as well, to catch another flight as to not further upset the passengers. I did and stumbled in my parents home around 0230 hours. I was finally home, but as I was to learn, it was not the same. Even in my home it was not the same as when I'd left a year and a half before. Things were different now and nothing I've experienced to this day has ever had the shine it did when I left. I'd done my duty, served my country and done so proudly, and received my "Welcome Home" aboard a National Airlines flight from LA to Houston.

    When I think back to that day, I still think about that man's question. "How many did you kill?" I wonder if he were standing in front of me today, what he would think when I looked him straight in the eye and told him that I am completely comfortable and take solace in my answer. None. My job as an FMF Corpsman was to save lives... and I did.

Speaking Out
by Staff Sergeant Ralph G. Schwartz

I first set foot on U.S. soil at Marine Corps Air Station, El Toro, south of Los Angeles. Then it was a quick cab ride to Los Angeles International Airport (LAX). The cab driver was a pretty decent sort-asked questions, such as if I was just getting back etc. He warned me about anti war protestors being at LAX, but I didn't think much about them, not then any way. When I got to LAX, I went in and got my ticket and headed for a barber shop. Spent a small fortune in the barber shop - shave, haircut, shoe shine, got my brass shined, uniformed pressed, etc. I was looking pretty sharp when I got out of there. The barber and his associates were pretty much like the cab driver-nice people. Then I headed for the terminal-it was like I entered a different world. Long haired dirt bags waving signs, depending on how you want to look at it, with the peace sign or the foot print of the American chicken, on them, chanting garbage about the vets, etc. Weird! Finally got out of there and arrived in Chicago. In less than a week, I went from seventy degrees (which felt cold in Vietnam) to twenty below in Chicago. It felt like I froze to death!!!!!!!!

Of course, having few clothes that fit, I wore my uniform everywhere. I put up with the bull shit from the protestors for a while, then decided to try to avoid them by not wearing my uniform. That got old real quick, and I started getting angry with the idiots. I put the uniform back on! Then when they approached me, I would get right in their face and dare them to do something, anything just to give me an excuse to smack them right in the mouth. The gutless wonders would always back down. The older folks, and especially the veterans of other wars, were usually pretty nice, or they just didn't say anything at all. The younger ones, well they were something else. They needed haircuts, an introduction to soap, and they needed a major transfusion of intelligence. I had no respect for them then, and like Jane Fonda, they are not welcome in my house to this day, not even on television. They fail to understand that Freedom is not Free and that it is the one thing you cannot have unless you are willing to give it to others.

I have heard it said (I know not by who) that "War is a terrible thing, but not the worst of things. Far more terrible is the man who stands for nothing and is willing to fight for nothing. He is a pitiful creature, made and kept free only by the efforts of better men then he." This is something that I have come to believe in and have always remembered. I have no use for the current crop of protestors either. They are, like their predecessors, a bunch of spoiled, ill-informed, pampered brats! The one thing I remember to this day is that when we came back, we no longer fit in with the others in our age group; they seemed so juvenile!

Have you ever seen a movie about Vietnam? I was there and I can tell you that none of them are accurate. They all contain three basic flaws.

1. They want to portray the war as black and white. As you have probably learned by now, there is very little in life that is black and white. Almost everything comes in various shades of gray. A classic example of this is the famous or should I say infamous picture of a Vietnamese General shooting a VC in the head. A whole lot was made of this picture by the media, but not one of them ever told the whole story. Yes, the Vietnamese officer shot the captured VC in the head, but what was not told was that the VC had just killed the General's entire family just before being captured. One must remember that many times in combat, justice is swift and usually takes the form of a bullet. I feel that the Vietnamese officer was more than justified in his actions, but you never heard any of this from the likes of Morley Safer or Walter Cronkite, neither of whom ever went out into the field. No, not them. They stayed in the relative safety of the rear and filed stories on things about which they had little or no knowledge. Another example of this is the South Vietnamese that we hired to unload the ships in DaNang. We paid him such a low wage that he was forced to steal from the docks and sell the items on the black market or to the VC just to feed his family. Was this right? What was worse, the low wage, his theft, or the sale to the VC? How about the little kid whose family was held hostage by the VC and he was told to go into an American compound with explosives tied to his back to blow them up, or they would kill his family. Of course I shot him.

Who was wrong? The VC? The little kid? Me?

2. It seems to me that the media, including the Hollywood elite, is very liberal and in many cases just plain leftists! They would have you think that the VC and the NVA were the good guys and that the United States was the bad guy. A good example of this is Hanoi Jane Fonda. If they love the communists that much and hate the United States that much, then why the hell don't they just move to a communist country and try to make a living there?

3. Literary license, or should I say Hollywood license. Many of the movies have elements of truth to them, such as John Waynes' "The Green Berets". The opening scene where the two Green Beanies are answering questions from civilians is a very good example of what I am talking about. This is accurate. Later in the movie they show VC atrocities which are also true (they only showed and/or mentioned the milder ones), the booby trap scenes are also accurate, but then they have to go and blow it by showing an NVA general being extracted by a C130 aircraft. Yes, this system exists, but it has never been used. It is just a shame that they have to embellish the truth to try to make a motion picture. What films are accurate? NONE. Which movies are fake? ALL of them to some degree.

If I could suggest a movie for others to watch to get a better understanding of the war, which one would I suggest? Not a one. Instead I would suggest that the individual take the time to sit down with a vet of this war, or any war, and just talk to them about it. You will learn more in thirty minutes than you will in an entire evening of Hollywood hype.

Sergeant Fred Hoekstra
By David "Doc" Forsyth

I first met Fred in 1969 when I became the Corpsman for Charlie Company First Tanks. I tried to get to know all the Marines for whose lives I had become responsible. Some were solemn and sober, but most were gung ho and ready to get at the enemy. There are always a few people who stand out in ones memory for whatever reason. Fred was not one of them. He was a tank mechanic for the company, one of those guys who did his job and did it well. He was responsible for keeping those M48 behemoths on the move, an enormous task that he handled with grace and professionalism. But if there is one thing that stood out about Fred, it was his indomitable spirit. He had a twinkle in his eye, a swagger to his gate, and a sincerity throughout his being that was infectious and inspiring. But the fact that he never made waves and did his job so well made him sort of disappear into the ether. My guess is Fred liked it that way. He picked his friends carefully and stuck by them ferociously. And for those of us who were fortunate enough to have been befriended by him, we found an incredible man with a rare, quirky sense of humor that surrounded us with constant laughter. Even when Fred was trying to be serious, you just couldn't help but laugh.

One of the things that Fred held deep inside was his desire to get into combat. After all, he was a Marine, and that is what he signed on for. It's not that he wanted to hurt someone, that was even a bit contrary to his basic nature, but he wanted to be tested. He wanted to be tested the way men have tested themselves since the beginning of time. He wanted, probably more than anything, to be a warrior.

I lost touch with Fred after he left Vietnam. Many years later, our Communications Sergeant at Charlie Company, and my good friend, Sergeant Gary D. Mefford sent me a Christmas card which included a snapshot of Gary and his wife and Fred and his wife. I did not give it a whole lot of thought at the time because Vietnam, thankfully, had become somewhat of a blur by then. I remember thinking it was good to know he was okay. Then, one evening many years later I received a call from a woman who said something like this, "Is this Doc Forsyth?" I wondered who this woman was who was calling me "Doc." That was a nickname strictly for Vietnam. "Well, we've never met but I believe you patched up my husband, Fred, back in Vietnam." The odd thing was that I did not remember patching up Fred, but I do know that he was awarded a purple heart, so it was a possibility.

Well, shortly after that, I got a call from Sergeant Mefford who had recently retired from his position as a school principal in Texas. Gary told me that he and his wife Margie were about to take a long vacation and travel around the country a bit, and one of the stops they intended to make was in Massachusetts to visit Fred and his wife, Beverly. It was at that time that I suggested that the four of them, Fred and Bev, Gary and Margie, arrange their trip to come through Washington, D.C. and I would meet them there. Done. That summer, nearly forty years after we'd parted company in Vietnam, we were reunited. It was wonderful. We visited the wall and experienced the power of that amazing monument. We shared pictures, stories, tears, and laughter. Fred was back in my life, and it was a joy. So much so that the three of us made a pact to return to the wall every November 11th for Veteran's Day. We honored that pact for years and extended the dates to include the 10th of November, the Marine Corps birthday, and always managed to include tours to the Smithsonian museum and all the monuments around that great city.

Fred's humor was still intact, the twinkle in his eye had remained, and it was wonderful to have become reacquainted. Our return trips started to expand in length and in the number of people who attended. We were able to find several more from our company, and everyone who was able joined us.

Fred was still very athletic, even after retirement from twenty plus years with the postal service. In fact, he had begun hiking the Appalachian Trail, and his goal was to do it in its entirety within two years - an admirable goal. Fred was an outdoorsman. He loved, and I mean loved, being out in the wilderness either hiking or paddling a canoe through remote waterways. When I learned this information, I suggested we do part of the Appalachian

Trail together. We decided that when he made it to Pennsylvania, I would join him and hike the trail with him for a while. We were set, or so we thought.

Fred was diagnosed with prostate cancer and had surgery. Then, he went camping about a week or so later just to "stay in shape." But the cancer had other ideas and decided it was not through with him. Fred battled that cancer every bit as hard, every bit as ferociously as anyone could ever expect from a Marine. And Fred was an exemplary Marine. If you were to look up the phrase "squared away" in your Marine Corps dictionary you would most certainly have found a picture of Fred.

Despite the surgery, the cancer battle raged on and his PSA continued to rise. Yet in spite of the pain and discomfort Fred was experiencing, he decided to take a couple of weeks and do another section of the Appalachian Trail. So he packed his gear and headed out from New York state to New Jersey heading south. I joined him in New Jersey and we hiked for several days through New Jersey and down into Pennsylvania camping along the way - a fantastic experience. Still growing weak from the cancer, he never complained and never let it get him down. I am so grateful to have had that time with him.

During one of the most difficult periods of his battle with cancer, Fred, his wife Bev, my girlfriend Deb, and I went camping and canoeing in the Adirondacks. It was by far one of the best trips I have ever been on. We laughed, paddled around lakes and streams, went fishing, set up a beautiful camp site, sat around the fire, read ghost stories, and laughed some more. Fred was in his element and loving it, even though he had become so very ill. The trip was nothing less than a testament to who Fred was. His soul resided in nature and he rallied there, but we had to leave. We had to go home at some point, and I wished we didn't. Three weeks later my friend Fred Hoekstra succumbed to cancer. But just a couple of days prior to his departure his "Nam Buddies" came to visit him in the VA hospital in Massachusetts. Gary Mefford drove 1,900 miles from Texas and Clyde Hoch and I came from Pennsylvania. This spoke to the bonds Fred had cemented into place with his friends. He was buried in a veteran's grave near his hometown of Agawam, Massachusetts. He was given a full Marine Corps military burial ceremony replete with a twenty one gun salute.

Fred finally did get into combat, and he fought valiantly. His war with cancer tested him to the extreme. Although he was defeated, he carried himself in a manner that made all who knew him proud. I miss him still.

Knowing Fred

By: Sgt. Gary D Mefford

I first met Fred Hoekstra in 1968 - shortly after TET. I was
transferred from 1st Tank Bn to assume the role of Charlie Company Communications Chief. Fred was a tank mechanic at our
cantonment at the end of the MSR just South of Marble Mountain.
We were both Corporals at the time. I had just lost a good buddy
(Russell L Wilcox) who was a radio communications operator with
a recon unit during that TET season in 1968 and I needed a good
friend to lean on for support. Fred became that person. We became
good friends very quickly. We hit our first disagreement early on.
When we talked about friendships, he made the negative, bold
statement saying that "You don't make friends in the Marine Corps
or Viet Nam – you only have acquaintances." We disagreed on that
and discussed that at length - many times! In later years, he has
told me that I became infuriated each time he said it.

Fred and I became good buddies, and we spent lots of time
together. We each had different responsibilities that took us different directions in our work and travels. He mostly worked at
company on tanks, but often did get sent out to platoons to resolve
tank problems. I had communicators assigned to various platoons
and often needed to travel to take radios, train crew members, or
relieve assigned communicators with replacements.

Fred was an organizer. I saw it first hand when he over-
hauled the entire tank maintenance record keeping system at
Charlie Company. It was in total disarray until Fred organized and
streamlined it. I was impressed with his personal filing system that
he maintained when we went to visit him in Massachusetts on July
4th of 2000. He pulled out various folders from those of us who
had corresponded. He had every Christmas card and letter I had
sent since we started in the 1970's. He arranged White House and
Congressional tours when we visited Washington DC. Later, he
arranged a trip for several to visit the Marine Corps Museum at
Quantico, and also the VIP seating for Veterans Day ceremonies at
the wall. Finally, he talked us into and arranged the Alaskan cruise
Fred, Bev, Margie, and I took May of 2008. Margie and I had

talked about an Alaskan cruise for 25 years and we were somewhat reluctant to go that year due to economic and time restraints. But, we are so pleased Fred finally talked us into pulling the trigger and going – it was a fantastic experience which we cherish.

Fred was also a mover and a shaker. He was into "Let's get R done" long before Larry the cable guy coined the phrase. Fred's favorite phrase was "Let's not dilly the dally!" He believed whole-heartedly in the meaning of that. He was always trying to move things and people along.

In Nam, having transportation to get to our platoons was always a hassle as Company had few jeeps at the time. So, I believe it was Fred who went with me to liberate one of those many "extra jeeps" the Army always seemed to have at the Army Supply Depot in DaNang. It was so easy to just drive into the depot and find one of those many jeeps. I hopped in one and drove out with Fred following me. No key needed-just the flip of a switch, guts galore, and a convincing story at the guard gate acting like I knew what I was doing and certainly had the authority to do it! We rushed back towards Marble Mountain and headed down the MSR towards Charlie Company. Since Fred was a tank mechanic, we set it up on tank road wheel sprockets and stripped it down. We removed all the Army paint, insignias, and numbers and painted it with the 1st Tk stencils and duplicated a number on another jeep in company. Fred and I then had our own jeep to come and go as needed-even though it was known as "C-28's jeep." Others also enjoyed the benefits of having "our own" jeep including Doc Forsyth, Sgt. Hoch, and others.

I decided to extend 6 months and talked Fred into it also. We had both gotten in country in December of '67 and since the Marine Corps had a 12 and 20 program, we would have the honor of spending two Christmases in Viet Nam. After experiencing TET of '68, I wanted to spend Christmas of 1968 at home. Extending for 6 months enabled us to go home for Christmas in 1968. We both did and both got telegrams at home, extending our Christmas vacations. Returning to country in January of 1969, we continued our friendship. My time in country came to an end August '69. I received orders to go back to MCRD San Diego as a communications instructor in C&E Bn. Fred and Doc took me to the airstrip in "my" jeep – how appropriate to have two good friends take me to the "Freedom Bird." We exchanged addresses and vowed to remain in touch.

The three of us maintained contact each year with a Christmas card and caught one another up on what the year had brought. Fred was in Massachusetts; Doc in either Florida, California, or New York; and we now lived in Texas. Fred and Bev came to visit us in 1989 - what a great reunion after 20 years of not seeing each other but maintaining that annual contact! Then, the three of us decided to meet in Washington DC the summer of 2000 and visit "The Wall" together. Doc had been there but Fred and I had not. What a tremendous reunion and very emotional visit at the wall. Fred was able to visit a buddy of his on the wall, and I was able to visit my good friend Russell Wilcox (Waynesfield, Oh) - who was also engraved in granite on that somber beckoning wall of stone. How awesome to have the support of two dear friends at this emotional experience. We jointly decided it would be appropriate to meet in DC for Veterans Day and the Marine Corps birthday so we began that tradition 2001.

I joined the VTA and was able to find another person I had searched for years – Sgt. Clyde Hoch. Now, Clyde became part of the group to meet annually in DC - among others for our reunion. Fred and Doc were both diagnosed with cancer and battled it courageously. We were all planning to attend the VTA reunion in Charleston in August. However, Fred continued to have setbacks in his battle and it became clear he would not be able to make it to the Charleston reunion. Then, we got the word that Fred would only have 1 to 2 weeks to live. We decided to change our plans and go to Massachusetts to see Fred one last time – instead of going to the VTA reunion. We (wife Margie and remodeling helper/"adopted son" Michael) towed our camper up that 1,933 mile journey to see a good friend – Fred. We had 4 days to visit. The first and last days were not particularly good for Fred. He was groggy from the meds and pretty non-responsive. However, the Saturday and Sunday in between were both blessings. He was alert, responsive, joking and we had a great time. Doc and Clyde both made it in that weekend and we had a great reunion at Fred's beside at the VA hospital.

It was difficult to leave but we needed to return home. We bid Fred good bye on Monday, July 20th. He had known who we were each time we visited him during our four days there. He seemed disappointed and saddened when I told him we needed to leave. We became emotional during our good-byes as we knew this would be our last time to see him. He commented on our getting all "choked up." On our return trip to Texas, I had a dream Tuesday night that he had died. Around noon on Wednesday, Doc called us as we were in Roanoke, VA to advise us that Fred had died during the night. We are so pleased we were able to make it up to see my good friend and enjoy one another's company one last time.

I bid you "farewell" my good friend, Fred. But, I do have to tell you that you were wrong - we both know that now! You don't have "just acquaintances" in the Marine Corps and Vietnam. These past 40 years have proven that theory wrong-you are and will always remain a good life-long friend, Fred. I will miss you and I thank God our paths crossed and I had the opportunity to know you all these years and be able to call you "friend!"

Your buddy,

Gary

Gary Mefford and Fred Hoekstra

Resources

United States of America 2000 Census

Veterans Administration: Study, 1995/National
Association of Chiefs of Police